From Violence to Resilience

Positive Transformative Programmes to Grow Young Leaders

Jo Broadwood and Nic Fine

Jessica Kingsley *Publishers*
London and Philadelphia

Quote from Richard Pascale on p.24 is reproduced by permission of Leader to Leader.
Quote from Adrienne Rich on p.46 is reproduced by permission of W. W. Norton. Copyright © 2002 by Adrienne
Rich. Copyright © 1978 by W. W. Norton & Company, Inc, from *The Fact of a Doorframe: Selected Poems* 1950–
2001 by Adrienne Rich. Used by permission of the author and W. W. Norton & Company, Inc.
Quotes from Nelson Mandela on p.84, p.115, p.147 and p.156 are reproduced by permission of the Nelson Mandela Foundation.
Quotes from Dr Robert Anthony on p.96 and p.101 are reproduced by permission of Dr Robert Anthony © 2011.
Quote from Helen Keller on p.183 is reproduced by permission of Random House, Inc. from *The Open Door* (1957).

Parts of this publication have been adapted from *Through the Walls: Working with Youth in Conflict, in Crisis, in Care, in
Custody* by Nic Fine, published in 1996 by Community Law Centre, University of the Western Cape, South Africa

Illustrations are by Alexander King, who successfully completed Leap's Young Trainers programme and now delivers courses for Leap.

First published in 2011
by Jessica Kingsley Publishers
116 Pentonville Road
London N1 9JB, UK
and
400 Market Street, Suite 400
Philadelphia, PA 19106, USA

www.jkp.com

Library of Congress Cataloging in Publication Data
Broadwood, Jo.
 From violence to resilience : positive transformative programmes to grow young leaders / Jo Broadwood and Nic Fine.
  p. cm.
 Includes bibliographical references.
 ISBN 978-1-84905-183-5 (alk. paper)
 1. Resilience (Personality trait)--Study and teaching. 2. Youth and violence--Psychological
aspects. 3. Leadership--Study and teaching. I. Fine, Nic. II. Title.
 BF698.35.R47B75 2011
 362.7083--dc22

                            2011013557

British Library Cataloguing in Publication Data
A CIP catalogue record for this book is available from the British Library

ISBN 978 1 84905 183 5

Printed and bound in Great Britain

Contents

Acknowledgements

We would particularly like to acknowledge the following people for their contribution to the development of the Leadership Programme and this guidebook.

- Alec Davison, Helen Carmichael and Jennifer Rogers, for their unfailing enthusiasm and commitment to ensuring the programme was properly developed and resourced.
- Governors, prison officers and managers at HMP YOI and RC Feltham, in particular Joe Whitty and Ian Telfor.
- Sue Jenkins, Michael Milton and Shane O'Sullivan from Westminster Young People's Services.
- All our delivery partners in the many different iterations of the programme across the UK.
- Leap senior trainers Jessie Ben-Ami (formerly Feinstein), Carey Haslam and Rene Manradge for adapting, developing and writing the materials for Chapter 9, 'Fear and Fashion'.
- Angela Hawke, Jennifer Rogers and Tom Currie for their feedback and comments.
- Especial thanks to Carey Haslam and Nik Pitcher for their careful reading, comments and support during the final editing process.
- Alexander King for his illustrations.
- Andy Kemp for helping to get permission to use the wide variety of quotes.

This guidebook is dedicated to all the young people who have participated in the Leadership Programme and who continue to be inspiring role models for their peers, their families, and their communities.

About the Authors

Jo Broadwood and Nic Fine were lead trainers for Leap in 1994, when they were responsible for the development of the original Leadership Programme with Feltham Young Offenders Institute. Nic was a co-founding member of Leap Confronting Conflict in the early nineties, and has authored several works focusing on youth and communities in conflict. He left the UK in 1997 to return to his homeland of South Africa, where he is the Director of Hearts of Men – a mentoring organisation which gives support to young men at risk of violence and gang activity, and mobilises older men and fathers to play an active role in their communities.

Jo Broadwood continued at Leap where she was responsible for the development of its action research programmes, including the 'Fear and Fashion' programme. She was also responsible for training practice and curriculum development, becoming the Director of the Leap Academy of Youth and Conflict in 2008. She left the Leap staff team in 2010, and continues to work as a specialist youth and community conflict practitioner.

Introduction

About this book

This is a guidebook for those working with young people at risk of violence: that is, young people who are caught in a cycle of destructive behaviour that harms their lives and the lives of others. The approaches described in this book build on 18 years of work by Leap Confronting Conflict with young people at risk. Originally developed and tested in a remand centre for young men awaiting trial, they can be applied to a much wider range of services for young people. The principles of programme design described here can be used by anyone developing a programme that aims to help young people transform themselves from community breakers into community makers.

From Violence to Resilience describes the structures, ideas, techniques and principles that have been used successfully with young people who are in conflict, in crisis, serving custodial or community sentences, under supervision or antisocial behaviour orders, or caught up in cycles of aggressive and violent behaviour. It does not provide easy answers or dictate the way in which to work with such young people. We hope, however, that it will act as a stimulus and support for those creating programmes to challenge, motivate and build resilience in the young people with whom they work.

Part One, 'Developing a Transformative Programme', is divided into five chapters:

- **Chapter 1: What is a Transformative Programme?**
  What constitutes a transformative programme? An outline of the background and the intention (the values and the purpose) that underpin the work.

- **Chapter 2: Preparing the Ground for Change**
  Developing local partners; the importance of local context, researching and auditing local conflict issues, and creating strategic alliances.

- **Chapter 3: Working with Young People**
  Recruiting your first cohort; the support young people need to attend a programme; the structure of the team and different team roles.

- **Chapter 4: Growing Young Leaders**
  How to develop meaningful roles for young people in communities, chart onward progression routes, and validate and accredit young people's learning.

- **Chapter 5: Gathering a Community of Support**
  How to work with partners, including dealing with obstacles, process and resource issues.

Part Two, 'The Leadership Programme', shares a comprehensive programme that has been delivered successfully in the community and in prisons with young people at risk. It is divided into four chapters; each chapter is focused on a three-day workshop. The Notes for Facilitators on page 53 provide guidance on facilitating the work.

- **Chapter 6: The Leadership Workshop**
  An introduction to the initial Leadership Workshop, followed by details for facilitating the three-day workshop programme.

- **Chapter 7: The Advanced Leadership Workshop**
  An introduction to the Advanced Leadership Workshop, followed by details for facilitating the three-day workshop programme.

- **Chapter 8: The Leadership in Action Workshop**
  An introduction to the Leadership in Action workshop, followed by details for a three-day peer facilitation training workshop and ideas for projects to consolidate and sustain the work.

- **Chapter 9: Fear and Fashion: Tackling Knife Carrying and Use**
  An introduction to a workshop on working with young people who carry and use knives, followed by details for facilitating the three-day workshop programme.

Who is this guidebook for?

It is for those who work directly with young people at risk of violence. It is also for those who manage and deliver programmes for young people within the voluntary and public sector Youth Services, Young Offender Institutions, Youth Offending Teams, Safer Neighbourhood Teams, crime reduction partnerships and housing and community associations.

It is also for those working at a senior and executive level to create and shape policy on working with young people in communities.

How to use this guidebook

- It can be used as a source of activities, exercises and ideas to complement your programme with young people.

- You could use it in its entirety with your programme, or select relevant parts of the different workshops.

- You could use the principles outlined in Part One to design your own transformational programme for young people.

While the programme was designed for young people at risk of violence, the concepts and frameworks apply to all conflict situations and are universal in their description of human thoughts, feelings and behaviours. The material is designed to be delivered by experienced facilitators who are already skilled in delivering group work programmes with young people at risk. The materials are aimed at young people aged 16 years and over. The content and delivery would need to be adapted for use with a younger age group.

The Leadership Programme in practice

- The Leap Leadership Programme was piloted in a remand unit at Feltham Young Offenders Institute and Remand Centre in September 1994, for one year. During that time, there was a reduction in the number of assaults on the unit. Young men who completed the Leadership Workshop went on to train as group facilitators in the weekly community meetings held on the unit. In addition, four members of the officer staff team were trained to support the workshop facilitators, support participants and lead the community meetings on the unit.

- In 1996, this work was incorporated into the work of the Community Law Centre at the University of the Western Cape in South Africa for eight months. It was also shared with South Africans and Namibians involved in juvenile justice work across the Western Cape in partnership with South African juvenile justice agencies.

- Elements of the programme were transferred back to the Feltham Remand Centre where the programme ran successfully for five years until 2001. The prison's Psychology Department carried out an independent assessment of young men completing the three-day Leadership Workshop. The results showed that after the workshop, young men demonstrated a significant reduction in levels of hostility and avoidance, and a significant increase in self-esteem.

- The Leadership Programme ran for a year from 1998 to 1999 on the young offenders' unit in HMP Rochester, and for two years from 2000 to 2001 with young women in HMP Holloway.

- Leap Confronting Conflict has used adapted versions of the Leadership Programme in the community since 2000, working in partnership with schools, the police, and youth service providers.

- Leap Confronting Conflict has been running the Leap 'Fear and Fashion' programme in partnership with Westminster Young People's Services since 2007. This project has adapted the Leadership Programme to support young people at risk of carrying and using knives. Young people are referred onto the programme by the Youth Offending Team (YOT) and the Positive Action for Young People team (PAYP). Young people completing the programme have gone back into education, or on to paid employment, and the programme has had a significant impact on re-offending rates.

- A Leadership Programme in Enfield from 2007 to 2010 resulted in 53 per cent fewer incidents of antisocial behaviour on one particular estate. Leap Confronting Conflict worked collaboratively with the police and other agencies to train both young people and the adults supporting them.

- At the time of writing, Leap is training and supporting officers in HMP Chelmsford to deliver the Leadership Programme to young men on remand.

Origins of the work

The programme reflected in this book was created through active research and development in the UK over many years. The ideas and resources have their roots in a wide range of sources, and draw on a number of different disciplines. It is, therefore, impossible to fully acknowledge all the individuals who have influenced and contributed to this work.

While Leap Confronting Conflict has developed this Leadership Programme, the content of workshops and exercises has been shaped and influenced not only by Leap's own practice, but also by knowledge and experience of the work of other organisations. We would like to praise and acknowledge the contribution of the following:

- the Alternatives to Violence Project
- the Geese Theatre Company
- Youth at Risk
- Augusto Boal
- the City Kids Foundation, New York
- Hearts of Men, South Africa.

Some of the materials included in this publication have appeared previously in *Through the Walls* by Nic Fine, published by the Community Law Centre, University of the Western Cape, South Africa in 1996.

Working with young people at risk

Risk is part of growing up. On their journey from childhood to adulthood, young people need to test limits, discover boundaries, explore the unknown and search for meaning and direction in their lives. What matters is the *level* of risk.

For some young people the risk can be life-threatening – to themselves, to others, and to people in their community. Caught up in dangerous and destructive behaviour, these young people have become used to a sense of power that is rooted in violence and aggression. Beneath the surface, however, there is often deep resignation and a sense of hopelessness, not only within themselves, but in their family and their community. Designing a programme that could make a real difference to these young people is a huge challenge. To do it, we need to look beyond the obvious – beyond their behaviour, the crime figures, their circumstances and background, important though these are.

The situation we face with these young people is much too serious to be ignored, and too complex for 'quick fix' easy solutions.

Transformative programmes

Many excellent programmes engage young people through activities such as sports, drama and music, and offer an alternative to spending time on the streets where they may be drawn into violent or criminal behaviour. These programmes are intended to *divert* young people away from crime and antisocial behaviour and can help them find new confidence, new skills and new friends. For some, this is enough to help them change the path they are on. These programmes can be an important first step in contacting and engaging young people who are traditionally seen as hard to reach.

However, there are many young people who are beyond the reach of such programmes. They are already cynical about life, or are so influenced by their peers that they find it impossible to break out of the life they are choosing. These young people are caught up in a vicious circle, and their families, local agencies, and the wider community often feel powerless to help them break out of that circle. They need a transformative programme – a programme that will help them change, fundamentally, the way they perceive themselves, the world around them and their place in their community.

Transformative programmes aim to obtain long-term results that are sustainable and transform the way in which young people live their lives. They build resilience in young people, giving them an opportunity to express themselves, and to reflect on who they are and what they do. Within a structured and facilitated process, young people are encouraged to examine themselves, their current choices, and the consequences of those choices. Ultimately, the young people *transform* themselves as the consequences of their choices become clear to them. They begin to develop a new, more resilient way of being in the world, and are aided by a community of support that is developed around the programme. Transformative programmes leave a legacy of young leaders who make an active and positive contribution to their community. This is the kind of programme described in this guidebook.

The vision and values of Leap Confronting Conflict

Our vision is a nation of young people who manage conflict constructively, and we believe that *all* young people are capable of this. We also believe that, very often, the young people who are the most caught up in conflict and violence are those with most to offer their communities. They have the most direct knowledge of conflict and violence, its causes and its consequences, and when trained as young leaders and facilitators they are the most convincing role models for other young people at risk. Our values are based on four core principles:

1. **Developing potential:** working for the best in yourself and in others. It means we are committed to recognising the potential in all young people and supporting them to be the best that they can be.

2. **Taking responsibility:** being accountable for your words and deeds, and taking responsibility for your choices and their consequences.

3. **Creating communication:** learning to speak honestly, acknowledging your feelings, your hopes, fears and needs. It is about expressing yourself to others in a way that is free from blame or manipulation, and that recognises the possible impact of your words.

4. **Building community:** developing relationships across differences in age, gender, ability, sexuality, race, faith or ethnicity. It is about recognising and valuing diversity and means, for instance, that Leap is proactive in modelling positive relationships across such differences in the teams that deliver its work.

Young people in communities

Many adults fear the kinds of young people who are recruited to Leap's Leadership Programme – they might describe them, for example, as 'professional destroyers', because they have a proven ability to destroy physical environments, property, relationships, and other people's sense of safety; they can hold an area or community in thrall, with others being afraid to speak against them or challenge them, for fear of reprisals and revenge; younger people may look up to them because of their perceived status and power, and their ability to win 'respect' from others; other young people may emulate their behaviour and look to them for leadership and guidance, which can create a vicious cycle within the community – the older young people effectively recruit younger people into their way of life and behaviour.

There is energy and talent here that can be transformed from a destructive ability to a creative ability. The Leap Leadership Programme gives young people the chance to find out what it is like to be part of a community project that actually benefits all those involved. Young people are welcomed into a new and alternative community. Here, in a structured programme, they are challenged and supported to confront their behaviour and find other ways to gain the respect and confidence of their peers. In the supportive environment of the programme they learn about responsibility, commitment, sharing, participation and being accountable for their actions. They develop skills for managing their thoughts and feelings. They understand the consequences of their words and actions and how to make positive choices. Through practising these skills they build personal resilience to enable them to resist conflict and violence. Through taking opportunities to contribute these new skills to others, they experience what it feels like to be acknowledged and affirmed in public. They begin to fulfil their potential and to discover what is possible in their lives.

They can then begin to transform their own views of themselves, and the way in which others view them and their potential. They can take on a new form of leadership in their community, where they become the diplomats, negotiators, fire-fighters, peacemakers, the community makers – helping other young people to make different, and better, choices.

Working in partnership

Leap Confronting Conflict is a specialist youth and conflict organisation. We provide skills training, with expertise in working with challenging young people, based on 18 years of experience in the design and delivery of transformational programmes for young people. However, we know, through experience, that no one organisation can transform a peer group or community. That kind of change needs organisations, agencies and the local community to work together to deliver structured interventions and support for young people. We work in partnership with communities, police services, young people's services, youth justice, schools and education services, community and mental health services and children's services throughout the UK, providing the specialist skills and resources to train young people in conflict awareness and conflict prevention skills. We also work with the adults in the organisations and communities that support those young people, providing the skills and knowledge that will help them intervene more effectively. Our local partners provide the ongoing support for individual young people, and the entry and exit points for the programme. They identify, refer and recruit young people, and provide routes for their future progress. Working in partnership, we can develop a critical mass of young people who have been through the programme and make an active contribution to their local community – a permanent legacy of young people who are transforming their own lives and the lives of others.

Part I
Developing Transformative Programmes for Youth at Risk

Chapter 1
What is a Transformative Programme?

To achieve all that is possible, we must attempt the impossible; to be as much as we can be, we must dream of being more.

Anon

What is a programme?

There is no correct answer to the question 'What is a programme?' A programme can be whatever we say it is, and its potential, or lack of it, is defined entirely by those who create and use it. This chapter sets out Leap's definition of a programme, based on ideas, structures and techniques that have been tested over 18 years of programme design for young people at risk.

The following list summarises our interpretation of what a transformative programme should be. You could add to it or create your own, and use it to guide you when creating a programme, and to check that the design includes all the necessary ingredients.

- A programme is transformative in its function.
- A programme is aspirational in its intention.
- A programme takes all who participate on a journey.
- A programme takes all who participate through a process.
- A programme is more than the sum of its partners.
- A programme is multi-focused in its practice.
- A programme provides a holistic approach to life.
- A programme provides an active experience.
- A programme is multi-dimensional in its scope.
- A programme leaves a legacy behind.

A programme is transformative in its function

Problems cannot be solved by thinking within the framework in which the problem was first created.

Albert Einstein

If we don't build the possibility of transformation into our programmes from the very beginning, we risk limiting their vision, their scope and their impact.

Many programmes for young people are 'corrective' – designed to respond to a specific problem. So we have programmes on 'anger management', 'bullying', 'offending behaviour', 'knife prevention' and 'tackling gangs'. Some succeed in addressing the specific problems but, while we see their value, they do not go far enough. They may solve the problems of a specific group of young people, but the conditions that created the problem in the first place still exist, and it will reoccur. We need to address the root causes of behaviour, as well as the immediate problem, and create the right conditions for young people to radically alter their approach to their own lives.

Transformation is very much an internal phenomenon that occurs at a particular point in time and in a way chosen by the individual themselves. It is a voluntary act. The approach of the Leap Leadership Programme, therefore, is not to 'correct' but rather to invite the participants on a journey across the barriers that they face, to take them beyond their limitations to a point where they can recreate themselves. It is an opportunity for them to alter the way in which they view themselves, other people and the world. The transformation process gives the young person critical choices, and facilitates the journey that emerges from those choices. When participants enter the process, they have already been 'created' by themselves and by their circumstances. The process of transformation gives them an opportunity to develop a new shape to their lives, to their relationships with themselves and with others. In doing this they alter their relationship to their past, their present and their future.

A programme is aspirational in its intention

> Shoot for the moon. Even if you miss, you'll land among the stars.
>
> Lester Raymond Brown

Much programme development is predicated on the question 'What's wrong?' If our programme only aspires to address what's wrong, we risk limiting its potential and its impact. A better question to ask ourselves might be 'What's missing?'

The design process of the Leadership Programme is a prime example. The programme was first developed in Feltham Young Offenders' Institute, which faced high levels of bullying and aggressive behaviour – an environment which had been blamed for the suicides of four young men in six months. Leap was asked to design and deliver a programme to address bullying.

Leap formed a design team with prison staff and carried out extensive interviews with young men and staff representatives. What was identified as being *wrong* was that young men were committing suicide because they could not cope with the hostile, unfriendly and unsupportive environment. However, defining what was wrong did not give the team a basis on which to design an effective programme.

Instead of looking at what was not working, the team began to look for what was *missing*. The answer was a sense of community in which people worked together to create a safe and friendly environment for all. Also missing were structured opportunities for young men to take responsibility and contribute to the life of the institution. It was clear that the leadership potential of the young men needed to be nurtured and developed. As a result, the team developed the idea of a leadership programme for the young men. Applying the term *leaders* to young men on remand was seen as fairly radical, but Leap believes in the potential of all young people to become leaders, for themselves, for their peers, and for their communities.

A programme takes all who participate on a journey

If you continue where you're going,
You will end up where you're heading.

Chinese proverb

If you are heading for trouble, you will get into trouble. If you are caught, you will end up in court. If you are heading for prison, you will end up in prison. Young people at risk often seem to be on a one-way collision course to further disaster. As mentioned, many programmes aim to *divert* young people away from experiences that could harm them and others. Diversion in this sense means a 'turning away' from something. For many young people a diversionary programme alone is enough. By being diverted through sport, drama, music, away from antisocial behaviour, petty crime, vandalism, they engage with new peers, form new friendships, develop a new passion or skills, and stop getting into trouble.

However, for some young people diversion is not enough. In order to truly transform themselves and their lives they also need to 'turn towards' something else. And after this 'turning towards' there needs to be a process of integration, a longer period of time during which young people incorporate and practise their experience and learning. This is the process of transformation.

Young people beginning this process must choose it for themselves. A magistrate or judge may order a young person to take part in a programme; a YOT team may refer a young person to a community-based programme. Everything may be in place. But the transformation process requires more than merely attending a programme and just sitting there. It works from within – being there – and comes from participating fully, as opposed to merely taking part. While we can make transformation a possibility, only the young person can make it a reality, by *choosing* it for themselves.

Transformation takes time, and is more effectively assessed and evaluated once a significant part of the process is complete. A year may be considered a realistic time-span to see measurable and sustainable results. The transformation process can be described as a journey, a travelling away from one world, and a moving towards another. It becomes real for young people when they experience it as a journey that occurs inside themselves. The longer the journey, and the bigger the gap between where the young person starts and where they end up, the more likely it is that the transformation will be permanent and sustainable.

The journey is essentially a personal development process. When a group of young people embarks on that journey together, it becomes a community development process.

A programme takes all who participate through a process

Life is not a having and a getting
But a being and a becoming.

Matthew Arnold

The journey includes the route and signposts on the way, and in our design of the journey we provide the map. The process describes what we will be 'doing' on the journey and includes exercises and techniques, facilitation style, programme structure, and guidelines for participation.

Key components of a process are:

- **joining:** going through the necessary steps in order to join the programme
- **belonging:** building a sense of ownership and belonging into the programme
- **listening:** creating an environment where people listen and are listened to

- **storytelling:** creating a space where people can share their life experiences
- **completing:** developing a process in which people can let go of past conflicts and move on
- **cooperating:** creating a community through common experience and combined action
- **exploring:** discovering how to continually improve and strengthen yourself
- **practising:** putting learning and new experiences into action
- **nurturing:** constantly checking on your own well-being and the well-being of others
- **supporting:** asking for, giving, and receiving support
- **acknowledging:** acknowledging what is and what is not working
- **achieving:** sharing your own achievements and those of others
- **recognising:** recognising the value of your contribution and the contributions of others
- **leaving:** going through the necessary steps to leave the programme
- **experiencing:** being able to experience all of the above in an active way and learn from that experience.

In Chapter 3, 'Working with Young People', we describe the process designed by the Leap team for the Leadership Programme.

A programme is more than the sum of its partners

> 'Never doubt that a small group of thoughtful, committed citizens can change the world; indeed, it's the only thing that ever has.'
>
> *Margaret Mead*

Programmes work best by bringing together a combination of resources that work together to produce results. When communities, organisations, departments, projects or agencies run their programmes in isolation, they are less able to serve young people.

Giving young people alternative resources is central to this work. They resort to violence when that is the only resource available to them, and when they feel they have no other way of communicating their anger and needs.

Reducing violence means giving our young people the resources that will equip them with the ability to find other ways of acting. This, in turn, will give them the potential to choose other options for themselves and to gain access to further resources.

A programme could draw on the following resources:

- **community:** involving community structures and support systems
- **volunteers:** involving people from local and surrounding communities
- **families:** involving parents, siblings, extended family and guardians
- **partnerships:** drawing on existing partnerships at local and regional level
- **professionals:** incorporating the experience and specialist skills of youth work professionals
- **organisations:** involving other youth- and community-orientated organisations
- **agencies:** providing access to employment, housing, health and education
- **business:** incorporating the experience and support of the business community

- **funders:** liaising with funding organisations and trust funds
- **politicians:** involving politicians in the promotion of the programme.

Working in partnership requires patience, transparency, clear partnership agreements, the ability to have difficult conversations about resources, power and differing organisational cultures, and a shared collective vision. See Chapters 2 and 5 for more details on developing partnerships.

A programme is multi-focused in its practice

Programmes need to reflect the complex nature of human beings. We rarely focus on only one thing, and are often trapped in – thinking about, worried about, dreaming about, longing for – the past, the present and the future, all in the same moment. A programme, therefore, needs to be multi-focused, to work with and distinguish between all three periods of time. Focusing only on the past, for example, would produce limited results, while focusing on the past *in relation to the present and future* has a far greater impact on how the individual understands their life experience.

The questions behind this multi-focused approach are:

- How can we learn from the past without being trapped in the past?
- How can we create a future that is not determined by the past?
- How can we bring our vision for the future into the present?

The questions to guide this exploration are:

- My past: who am I (and what got me here)?
- My present: where am I (and what's keeping me here)?
- My future: where am I going (and where else could I go)?

These questions form the basis of the Leadership Programme, and in particular the Leadership and Advanced Leadership Workshops. (See Part 2 of this guidebook for examples of practical work using these questions.)

A programme provides a holistic approach to life

Values are caught rather than taught.

Anon

A programme works best when everything around it reflects its internal values and intention. A programme is weakened if it runs in isolation from the environment around it, or when that environment actually contradicts its values and intention – such as a peer mediation programme in a school where staff shout at or belittle students.

The ultimate success of the work rests on how holistic it is, and on how successfully it is integrated into the different facets of a young person's life. Its success also depends on having as many people as possible living and practising the values of the programme alongside the young person.

The Leadership Programme is designed to be as holistic as possible, and to involve partners, managers, staff, volunteers, the wider community and youth in its processes. It occurs within a community and group process, not in isolation. It involves training, practical application, involvement in community life, and opportunities for initiative.

A programme provides an active experience

It's easier to act your way into a new way of thinking than think your way into a new way of acting.

Richard Pascale

The programme has to be experienced in person to have an impact – it cannot be taught, lectured or preached. By creating a journey and a process for the participants, the programme provides an experience in which there is an opportunity for learning, self-discovery and personal development. The programme uses active techniques such as drama and role-play to support the learning of participants, and help them rehearse the skills and strategies they are developing. This helps them move from 'head' knowledge to 'whole-self' knowledge, where the feelings and emotions, the body and nonverbal communication can be engaged alongside thinking and reasoning.

The immediate short-term function of a programme is to intervene in the lives of young people at risk. During this period they have an opportunity to alter their view of themselves and extend their options, making choices, where before there was only 'one way'. They get to see that their past echoes their present, and will be re-echoed in their future. They begin to understand the link between the past and the present, and to see how the future will be the same if they do not change the pattern. They start to learn how to act differently, so that they can leave the past – and its restrictions – in the past. This gives them access to a future which they can choose to create, rather than one that gets created for them. They examine their assumptions about themselves; they express their feelings and speak about things that they have been unable to speak about before.

The medium-term function of the programme is to enable the participants to make full use of this learning in their everyday lives, and to begin to integrate a new way of being by taking on a public role in their community that requires them to develop their new skills further.

The long-term function is to deepen the process of integration. The young people work on building a future for themselves, learn how to deal with mistakes and disappointments, experience alternative ways of dealing with conflict, gain essential working skills, continue with their education or training, and build personal resilience, confidence and independence.

A programme is multi-dimensional in its scope

Human beings have many dimensions that shape their character and their personality, and programme design needs to take all of these into consideration. You can apply the 'spice of life' checklist to ensure that all human dimensions are included in the programme design:

Social – **P**sychological – **I**ntellectual – **C**ultural – **E**motional.

Each dimension is underpinned by an associated quality:

Spiritual – **P**otential – **I**nspiration – **C**ommunity – **E**xpression.

If a programme contributes in some way to each of these dimensions and qualities, it is treating the person as a whole, rather than isolating a specific part of their being.

The checklist opposite gives us a powerful framework to engage with young people, and strengthens the design of the Leadership Programme.

The SPICE of life checklist

Dimension: SOCIAL

How we relate to people – to groups – to others
Relating – communicating – cooperating

Quality: SPIRITUAL

Developing a sense of self – of spirit
Living with a purpose in life

Dimension: PSYCHOLOGICAL

How we think about ourselves – others – situations – family – community
The impact our thoughts have on ourselves – our choices – our actions

Quality: POTENTIAL

Believing in our own potential
Living in a world full of possibility

Dimension: INTELLECTUAL

Thinking creatively – discovering – exploring – investigating – inquiring
Developing an interest in life – questioning – reasoning – identifying

Quality: INSPIRATION

Living a life – with intention – with commitment – with direction
Being awake – being alive – having a passion for life

Dimension: CULTURAL

Valuing cultural roots – that which connects us – that which bonds us
Developing a sense of history – of identity – of togetherness

Quality: COMMUNITY

Experiencing being in community – with ourselves – with others
Living in a supportive environment – giving support – receiving support

Dimension: EMOTIONAL

How we feel about – ourselves – others – family – the world
The impact our feelings have on ourselves – our choices – our actions

Quality: EXPRESSION

Expressing ourselves fully – with confidence – with freedom
Acknowledging and communicating our emotions – to ourselves – to others

A programme leaves a legacy behind

The solution to adult problems tomorrow depends on large measure upon how our children grow up today.

Margaret Mead

Young people who have been through a transformative programme have a sense of their true potential and the huge contribution they can make to other young people. They are often imbued with a sense of urgency and a mission to ensure that other young people in their local community do not get caught up in the same destructive behaviour that they are leaving behind.

To leave a lasting legacy the programme must capture and harness this sense of purpose and agency by creating multiple opportunities for young people to influence, mentor and role model an alternative way of dealing with youth conflict and violence. Encouraging and supporting these young people with volunteering, employment and training opportunities develops a pool of young leaders in the local community who are educating and leading others; a *critical mass* of young people who are active in building a more peaceful and harmonious community. A programme can change a local area from being one with high levels of antisocial behaviour and youth-on-youth violence, and where local residents are fearful of young people, to one where violence is the exception, where young people lead the way in promoting community relations, and where people feel a sense of belonging and pride.

There are four essential components to Leap's transformative programmes:

- preparing the ground for change
- work with young people
- growing young leaders
- developing a community of support.

These are explored in more detail in the following chapters.

Chapter 2
Preparing the Ground for Change

Another word for creativity is courage.

George Prince

The process of designing a new programme is a creative act. The potential of the programme depends on how much the designers use their imagination and inspiration, dream of what is possible, and go beyond their limitations, obstacles and difficulties. If we examine programmes that achieve extraordinary results, we find that they are often built on what is at first considered a 'crazy idea', an approach that is uncomfortable, or a suggestion that challenges a way of thinking and doing.

The first stage, preparing the ground, is about *defining* and *designing*. In this stage we:

- identify the broad scope of the programme – *its breadth*
- focus on aims and intentions – *our vision*
- design the overall structure, style and content – *our methods*.

Identifying the scope of the programme – its breadth

Answers to four questions help us to identify potential partners in the creation, development and delivery of the programme:

- Who has initiated the invitation to develop a programme?
- What is the profile of the participants?
- Where is the programme to be located?
- What is the scope of the programme?

Sometimes the answers can be very straightforward. For example, Leap was invited by a funder to develop a programme within a prison where four young men had committed suicide in the past six months. It was relatively easy to define the partners: the funder and the prison.

Sometimes it is more complex. Leap's 'Fear and Fashion' programme, for example, originated with a consortium of funders. The consortium had already initiated research into why young people carried and used knives, after a number of fatal stabbings of young people by other young people. The consortium now funded four model projects to develop innovative approaches to knife carrying and weapon use. Leap was asked to locate its programme in an inner-city London borough that was badly affected by knife crime. The first task was to engage with local agencies and the community, to develop a local partnership that would oversee and support the entire programme. Partners included the Youth Service, the Youth Offending Team (YOT), a local school, the police service, the Youth

Council, and the education service. However, there was also a wider strategic partnership around the programme, consisting of the funders, an advisory board, the external evaluators, and the other three model projects.

Together, these agencies and the potential participants would create a 'stakeholder map'. We suggest that developing this map very early in the process will pay benefits later, ensuring that the programme is located firmly within current best practice, linked to local priorities and established work, and has access to resources to better meet local needs.

Focusing on aims and intention – the vision

Two questions are important here:

- What is the problem?
- What is missing?

Identifying and articulating *what is wrong* is an important first step in creating the aims and intention of the programme. But addressing only what is wrong can limit the vision of the programme. If we also ask *what is missing*, it helps us to define what the programme might help create or develop.

With Leap's 'Fear and Fashion' programme, for example, the answer to '*What is wrong?*' is the problem of increased knife carrying and weapon use amongst young people. If we stop there, we are likely to create an *anti-knife* programme with a narrow focus on diverting young people away from knife carrying and use. This may not address the underlying issues that lead young people to carry knives in the first place. Deepening the exploration by asking '*What is missing?*' points us towards these underlying themes.

The following emerged as 'missing':

- young people feeling safe on the streets and in their communities
- skills for dealing with low-level conflict to prevent its escalation
- enough young people who are positive role models for others
- information and awareness of the dangers of carrying a knife
- young leaders who can teach others about the dangers of knife carrying and use
- enough structured opportunities for young people to take leadership on this issue within their community
- young people feeling respected and valued by the community.

This broader answer helped us to build a stronger vision for the programme.

This vision needs to be created with partners and stakeholders, and particularly with young people. By engaging people in questions on what is wrong and what is missing, we start to build momentum, enthusiasm and direction for the programme. Partners begin to identify the possible benefits for themselves, and for their service users, and how they can contribute. The programme starts to become collectively owned.

One of the most effective methods Leap has developed to build that collective ownership is an initial *conflict audit* or conflict survey. A wide group of potential stakeholders identifies and articulates the underlying issues and imagines what is needed to tackle it effectively. Information, opinions and views are collected through audit/survey forms, focus group interviews, and interviews with key players, and the results are summarised, analysed and written up into a report.

Young people are at the heart of this process, and it is important to interview and consult those who are directly involved and affected by conflict and violence, as well as those who are bystanders, witnesses, and audiences for conflict.

Depending on the scope and breadth of the programme, other stakeholders in the conflict audit/survey might include:

- teaching staff and school support staff
- youth workers – in the YOT, Youth Service, police, etc.
- staff and managers of local services
- parents
- community members
- local business
- local politicians
- funders.

The results can be illuminating and allow people to see the problem differently. One head teacher described the report as 60 per cent information he already knew, 25 per cent information that he knew but had stopped seeing because it was so familiar, and 15 per cent completely new information. Being reminded of things you have stopped seeing gives you a fresh impetus to take action. The new information can identify a hidden issue or problem that reveals important insight. The pupil survey responses, for example, may highlight variations in how different ethnic groups feel they are treated in school, enabling schools to address this through targeted activities and interventions.

Designing structure, style and content – our methods

The four questions to be answered are:

- How can we deliver the vision and desired outcomes of the programme?
- What are the structures that will help us deliver it?
- Is what we are designing aligned with our stated values?
- What are the style and content that will help us achieve our aims?

In designing the Leadership Programme for Feltham Young Offenders and Remand Institute, the Leap team used the guidelines outlined in Chapter 1: 'What is a Transformative Programme?' They developed a vision statement for the programme and expressed the foundation stones – the *core beliefs and values* behind the work – and the cornerstones – the *fundamental aims* of the programme.

- The programme is *action-oriented*. The workshops, groups, and meetings all provide the young person with an active experience from which to learn.
- It is *inclusive* and encourages active participation. It is designed to make an impact on the whole system, and not to operate in isolation.
- It seeks out and *expects the best* of all the young people who participate.

- It creates the conditions for an *intervention* in their lives.
- It gives them an *opportunity* to practise the skills that they have learnt, and to integrate them into their daily lives.

They then worked on creating the overall programme structure. The Leadership Workshop described in Chapter 6 would be an entry-level workshop open to all young men on the unit. Those who made good progress at the workshop would be invited onto the Advanced Leadership Workshop outlined in Chapter 7. This, in turn, would make them eligible for the Leadership in Action workshop (Chapter 8), which would train them as group leaders. At each stage there would be built-in opportunities for them to practise their new skills, culminating in their leadership of small groups during the unit's weekly community meetings.

The team worked up this broad framework within the guidelines, and then created the appropriate structure for each part of the programme, ensuring that the aims and values were reflected throughout. The building blocks and key statements, together with the audit results, also formed the basis for the selection and design of appropriate detail and content for the workshops. This framework also gave the team and partners a reference point and focus for the entire period of delivery.

The team used images and metaphors that would capture the imagination and the energy of the young people. The titles used for the exercises, for example, include: 'Bombs and Shields', 'Playing with Fire', 'Power Game', 'Getting Hooked', 'Dangerous Journey', 'Jailbreak', 'Red Labels', and 'Personal Destroyers'. They selected a facilitation style that would be challenging and supportive, tough and understanding, and firm yet flexible.

The careful development of a collaborative and creative partnership approach that can deliver the desired outcomes is vital to the definition and design of the programme. A broad-brush project plan can be developed to take account of the programme structure and sequencing, and to include all stakeholders, and determine when to consult and engage them, and when to simply include or inform them.

The initial work around scope and vision to prepare the ground takes time and patience, but Leap believes that it is crucial. Neglecting this stage makes it likely that trouble will occur further down the line. The team leading the process needs to listen hard to what is being said (and sometimes to what is not being said) by young people, and by the different stakeholders and partners. The team needs to engage and enthuse others in the idea of the programme, and begin to plan for the sometimes tricky issues involved in engaging partners with different agendas, resources and power. They need to build the strongest of foundations to maximise the likelihood of success.

> *If you have built castles in the air, your work need not be lost; that is where they should be. Now put the foundations under them.*
>
> *Henry David Thoreau*

The Leadership Programme

Vision statement

We intend to create a programme that will develop the **leadership potential** within every participant in order for them to become **contributing members** of their **communities** (be they a young person, a paid member of staff, or a volunteer)

The programme will promote:

- taking responsibility
- making commitments
- realising potential
- giving and receiving support.

Foundations

The Leadership Programme will be built upon certain core **values and beliefs**, which will be reflected at all levels of activity:

- individual respect – recognising that every human life is valuable
- no violence – commitment to resolving differences and disputes without violence
- democratic process – freedom to participate and make well-informed choices
- creative potential – encouraging full self-expression and opportunity for growth.

Cornerstones

In the Leadership Programme our **aim** with all participants will be to:

- enhance self-confidence – through their self-worth, self-belief, self-esteem, self-concept and self-image
- increase levels of communication – through an appreciation of the power of their listening and of their speaking
- build a sense of community – through their commitment, trust, respect and participation
- work creatively with conflict – through their awareness, understanding and skill development.

The Leadership Programme (*continued*)

Building blocks

In the Leadership Programme we will focus on **developing key areas** which will **enable participants** to take a lead in their own lives:

- people **listening** to themselves and each other
- people **exploring** who they are, and how and why they do things
- people **taking action** and control in their lives
- people **gaining personal power** – being responsible for themselves and making informed choices
- people **supporting each other** – by giving and receiving support.

Statements focusing on taking a lead in life

- If you don't **stand** for something – you will fall for anything.
- If you don't **choose** for yourself – others will choose for you.
- If you don't **do** it yourself – others will do it for you or do it to you.
- If you don't **create change** – change will create you.

If you don't **take responsibility** and you hold others responsible, blaming them for your life, your behaviour and your destiny, you will never have the **power** to shape your own destiny. The **power** will always live with others and not with you, will lie outside you and not within you.

Chapter 3
Working with Young People

A ship in harbour is safe,
but that is not what ships are built for.

William Shield

This phase is both tough and exciting. Now we test the programme design in practice and see what it looks like in reality. With our partners we move from paper, from discussions and planning meetings, to the real world of success and failure, joy and sorrow, enthusiasm and resistance. In this phase you have to hold your course in the face of those who look for instant results, or those who claim 'I told you so' at the very first obstacle. We have to steer the ship out of the harbour for the first time, and the waves and the winds will challenge our vessel at every stage of its journey.

This phase is about *delivering* and *developing*. In this stage we:

- create the programme within space and time – *its physical presence*
- bring the design to life with facilitation and participation – *our practice*
- refine the delivery of style and content through review, testing and feedback – *our experience.*

Creating the programme within space and time – its physical presence

Recruiting and delivering to young people

The programme needs to reflect a positive and dynamic image in its title and content. Young people at risk are not used to being referred to as young leaders, or being seen as having the abilities and skills to lead others.

The first cohort needs to be recruited carefully. Key frontline workers from the local partnership can play a crucial role, as they already have relationships with the young people. These workers will need to be enthused about the programme. Sometimes a conversation or presentation is enough, but it is also effective to share past results, evaluations and testimonies with them, and, if possible, give them an opportunity to see the programme in action.

The first cohort is always the hardest to recruit, but is worth a significant investment of time and effort. It becomes progressively easier, as the first participants will usually recruit those that follow. This can happen naturally, through their conversations with friends and peers, and very effectively through their leadership of taster sessions or open evenings for other youths. Key workers can also put potential participants in touch with young people who have completed the programme.

Encouraging attendance

The Leadership Programme has been delivered in many different contexts and with many different partners. Much can be made of the importance of participants choosing to attend voluntarily, but in reality they will attend for a variety of reasons. One particular Youth Service paid young people to attend. The amount paid was relatively small and consisted of vouchers, but it got them into the training room. In prison, young people attended to get out of their cells for the day. Young people may be strongly encouraged or referred by a judge or a probation officer or a YOT worker.

The job of the facilitation team is to ensure that, whatever their reason for attending on Day 1, they come back on Day 2 because they have started to see the possibilities of the programme. Ultimately the facilitator's role is to engage participants (and to keep them engaged) in an exploration of their ability to create a different future for themselves and to change their current path. We find this has an intrinsic value that far outweighs any other motives for attending. By the end of one programme, for example, young people who were initially paid to attend acknowledged that the vouchers had motivated them to attend initially, but that the experience had given them far greater benefits than the amounts paid to them.

The profile and suitability of participants

We recommend that potential participants have individual interviews with the workshop facilitators and support staff. These individual interviews are an opportunity to explore the possibilities offered to young people by participating in the programme. It is also the time to discuss any issues around participation, such as attendance, participation, safety, security and confidentiality; and to talk through any practical support that is needed in terms of travel, venue, childcare, etc. Young people need to be able to commit to full attendance to workshops and any follow-up sessions – it must be clear that this is not a 'come and go as you please' workshop.

At this stage we recommend careful thinking about the make-up of the group. It may be worth recruiting a mixed group, including individuals who exhibit very challenging behaviour, and others already engaged in peer leadership activities. The latter can act as informal supports and enablers for those who are more likely to struggle with challenging behaviour during the training. Putting the most challenging young people together in one exclusive group can be counterproductive and undermine the impact of the training. Careful thought is needed on whether this is going to be a mixed-sex group. For example, young women (and young men) may participate better and feel more comfortable in a single-sex environment, particularly if there are issues in the local area around gang membership and affiliation. Consideration should also be paid to issues of territory, ethnicity and culture in the local community, and whether they might impact on participants' behaviour and group tension. For example, in some contexts it may be preferable to work in mono-ethnic groups in the early stages of the programme, bringing young people from different ethnic backgrounds together when they have developed greater understanding and skills for managing conflict.

Numbers of participants

We advise a high facilitator to young person ratio, given the intensity of the training and the kind of young people involved. This allows for some flexibility in the facilitation team and for facilitators to be available for individual conversations with young people who are struggling. We recommend no more than 12 participants, with careful risk assessment and using experienced and advanced facilitators.

Security and safety issues

Individual risk assessments should be carried out on all young people attending the programme. Rules around remaining drug- and alcohol-free and, for instance, carrying weapons, need to be established in the initial participant interviews, and then reinforced as the programme is delivered. A risk assessment of the entire programme should be carried out in the early stages and any wider community safety concerns addressed. For example, is the programme likely to bring together young people from rival territories or gangs? Security and safety issues need to be monitored throughout the entire life of the programme, and the level of risk for individual participants reassessed at regular intervals, from their attendance at their first workshop through to the stage when they are delivering workshops in the local community.

Policy around confidentiality

The Leadership Programme encourages self-revelation and reflection as an essential part of the process for participants. During the process a participant may reveal that they have been the perpetrator, witness or victim of a crime of which key workers were previously unaware. They may reveal that they have been, or are being, physically harmed or sexually abused. It is important that the local partnership agrees a policy on what is confidential and what is not, in line with their statutory responsibilities, before the first workshops, and that this policy is widely shared with staff from partner organisations to ensure consistency. This policy needs to be made clear to participants in the initial interviews and reiterated at key points during the programme so that they are aware of the possible consequences of sharing such information.

Pastoral care for young people

We would recommend that the facilitation team and the support staff work closely with each other over the course of the programme, to monitor and support individual participants' emotional and mental well-being. Key workers and staff from the partnership agencies will be best placed to offer pastoral care and support, as they will have an ongoing relationship with individual participants. If possible they should be available at the end of workshop sessions for some informal time with participants, or to offer individual support. They should also be able to refer young people on to appropriate services where necessary, for example housing, benefits, pregnancy and contraception advice, domestic violence, etc.

The logistics

Practical details around the delivery of the workshops will need to be discussed. For example: how often will workshops be held? Where will they be held? Is the location going to prevent any participants attending? Will they, for example, have to travel through potentially hostile or unsafe territory to get there? How long will the days be? When will they start or end? Will a prayer room be needed? Will lunch be provided? Our experience is that if young people leave the workshop environment for lunch and return to their usual environment, whether that is the wing of a prison, the school playground, or the street, it increases the amount of time it takes to settle them back in and re-engage them for an afternoon session.

It is important that the logistics of the workshop itself work smoothly, so establish whether equipment such as flip chart, marker pens, materials for games and activities, will be provided by facilitators, the venue or partners.

Staffing the programme

There are huge benefits to having local key workers experience the workshops alongside their young people. The key workers have an ongoing, day-to-day relationship with young people, and their support and commitment to those completing the programme is vital, as they will have shared the journey and had an opportunity to deepen their relationship. Involvement in the workshop will provide key workers with personal and professional development training, as they learn the tools and techniques to help young people deal with conflict and violence more constructively. They will develop a deeper understanding of what challenges and motivates a young person's behaviour, and gain insight into some underlying issues, which can form a basis for one-to-one support and coaching of the young person throughout the programme.

It is essential that the role of support staff, such as key workers, is explored and agreed during the 'define and design' stage of the programme, so that senior managers are aware of, and committed to supporting, the extra demands on the time and resources of these frontline staff. The issues that may need to be addressed are:

- gaining staff support for the programme
- scheduling of staff, rosters, hours, etc.
- staff incentives – e.g. training, accreditation
- predicting and managing the strain of the programme on other core activities
- planning and preparation time for key workers.

Monitoring, evaluation and review

Now is the time to establish an evaluation plan and to agree who is responsible for it. The plan should be incorporated into the programme framework and all processes should be in place before the start of the live programme itself. It should be agreed who is taking overall responsibility for summarising and analysing data and producing the required reports, and who is responsible for collecting monitoring and evaluation data. The partnership will need to consider such questions as: How will the programme be monitored to ensure that it is reaching its original target group? How will you demonstrate that the programme is achieving its aims and objectives? What short- and long-term evaluation methods can be built into the fabric of its delivery?

The evaluation plan could include, for example, the collection of baseline data from the individual participant interviews and the conflict audit/survey; individual and group evaluation of sessions and workshops; longer-term follow-up on past participants; mapping progression routes; and additional relevant data collected through the partner agencies, such as local antisocial behaviour and crime statistics, participants' re-offending rates, community well-being and resilience measurements. If funds are available, an external evaluator could be appointed.

Bringing the design to life with facilitation and participation – our practice

Like the participants, facilitators also go on a journey of self-discovery and growth. To deliver this work, you need to *be* the work, you need to walk the talk, providing a role model to young people, key workers and partner agencies of constructive, creative and skilful ways of dealing with conflict, difficulties and challenging behaviour. You need to be a leader, a facilitator, a guide, and a fellow traveller. Young people will challenge and inspire you and take you to your learning edge. They will test your knowledge, your ability to hold tough conversations, and to navigate surely through tricky terrain. This is just as it should be.

You will see that the Leadership Programme materials are complex and layered in order to achieve change and transformation. They are designed to be delivered by experienced, advanced facilitators. Care is needed in choosing and preparing the team to achieve the right balance of diversity and strengths, style and experience.

We recommend that you plan and prepare carefully as a facilitation team, allowing time for meaningful team planning, preparation, review and reporting. We strongly recommend that formal briefing and debriefing sessions are integrated into the programme, timetabled after each session throughout the entire delivery. Extra time should also be allocated for partnership meetings, discussions and informal contact time. In addition, facilitators may need external support and supervision in order to learn from the themes and issues that emerge out of delivering the work in order, to improve and develop their practice.

In their first team planning sessions the Leap team spent time considering the *journey* that the young people would be taking, and the *process* that they would go through. Building on the *vision, foundations, cornerstones* and *building blocks* developed in the design process gave the team and the participants a sense of where they were heading. The journey and process statements developed for the Leadership Programme can be seen on pages 38–39.

Refining the delivery of style and content through review, testing and feedback – our experience

We have now completed the define, design and delivery phases. We have defined what the programme is by creating the intention; we know what it looks like because we have created its overall shape and content; and we have started to see how it functions in practice. Now we must develop the programme, as it will experience obstacles, its facilitators will face challenges, and there will be those who resist its progress and even attempt to undermine it. While keeping faith in the original vision statement, the facilitators need to commit themselves to the continual improvement of the programme – the best way to strengthen its implementation and motivate all its supporters.

The development of the programme could consist of a process of redefining objectives, redesigning content and structure, and enhancing the way in which the programme is being delivered. Alternatively, the development phase could consist of merely fine-tuning these elements. Again, we focus on what is *missing* in the programme rather than what is *wrong* with it. Some things will work and some things will not. The programme has a commitment to develop *all* those people who participate in it – the facilitators, apprentice trainers, youth leaders or volunteers, community members and support staff, as well as the young participants.

Sometimes it is key relationships within the staff team or within partnerships that need to be developed, rather than the content of the programme or the training of personnel. These relationships can make or break the process of building a new programme. All these relationships need ongoing care, attention and work.

So *continuous development* is a commitment built into the very heart of the programme, which should be reflected in all its components. Sometimes those taking part may feel the strain and extra work involved in establishing, maintaining and developing a transformative programme. It is crucial for the partners and project manager to involve, inform and acknowledge all stakeholders and contributors so that they are motivated to keep on developing the work. Assuming that what works now will always work is a fatal mistake for longer-term sustainability!

Our greatest glory is not in never failing, but in rising every time we fail.
Confucius

The Leadership Programme

Key components of a journey are:

The starting point

Knowing what is going on in the lives of the young people – knowing what state they are in when they enter the programme – knowing where to begin.

The destination

Knowing where we intend to get to on completion of the journey – knowing where this particular journey is heading – knowing the purpose of a particular journey.

The signposts

Knowing each stage of the journey – knowing what can be expected from each stage – knowing when we have arrived and when we need to proceed.

The people

Who is coming on the journey as participants, facilitators, coaches, or supporters – knowing the function of each person undertaking the journey.

The safety net

Knowing what is needed in order to complete the journey – creating necessary support systems – creating an environment in which the programme can work.

The resources

Besides human resources and the environment, knowing what equipment, space, physical surroundings, accommodation, clothing and food are needed.

The preparation

All that needs to occur before departure – the training, the planning, the agreements, the understanding, the commitments, the information.

The compass

Last but not least, having a place to which you can always return for direction, focus, comfort, rest, inspiration and energy. This place is the heartbeat of the programme, it keeps the journey process on track.

The Leadership Programme

The process

Unlocking the **present** from the **past** to create a **future**.
In the Leadership Workshops each participant will be **taken through a process**

The present – taking stock

- taking stock of ourselves in the present – who we say we are
- looking at our relationships – reacting versus responding
- examining how we communicate – listening to ourselves and to others.

The present – unpacking the punch

- looking at how we do what we do
- examining what sparks us – expressions of upset and anger
- understanding our reactions in situations of conflict with ourselves and others.

The past – cracking the act

- exploring who we are and why we do what we do
- Who am I? What's got me here? Where am I? What's keeping me here?
- exploring roots of anger, rage and aggression.

The past – breaking out

- putting the past into the past – informed by the past and not constrained by the past
- taking action and control in our lives – moving away and moving towards
- Where am I going? Where else could I go? What do I need to get there?

The future – taking a stand

- being responsible for our lives and creating opportunity
- making our own choices in life
- sharing ourselves with others – full self-expression.

The future – moving on

- asking for and receiving support from others – offering and giving support to others
- commitment to staying in communication with others
- extending the boundaries – the set limitations of our thinking.

Chapter 4
Growing Young Leaders

> *The real act of discovery consists not in finding new lands, but in seeing with new eyes.*
>
> Marcel Proust

Our first cohorts of young people are now trained in the first stages. The relationship between partners is established and strengthened as all begin to see the evidence of change in the young people. Others hear about this and begin to see the potential of the programme for the wider community around it. The young people have begun to develop a new sense of possibility.

Now their energy and enthusiasm, their new skills and understandings, need to be channelled, so that they can *consolidate* their learning by integrating their workshop experience into their daily life. They will need clear progression routes, and encouragement and support from key workers to keep moving towards the personal goals they have developed. They need opportunities to *demonstrate* the changes in their thoughts and beliefs, their words and actions, to their families, to their peers, to the wider community, and most of all, to themselves.

This component is about consolidating, *progressing* and *demonstrating*:

- creating the legacy on which to build the future of the programme
- showing it works – tracking and proving the changes to realise and showcase outcomes.

Creating the legacy on which to build the future of the programme

It is important to:

- create opportunities for young people to practise their skills
- use existing structures and activities to develop young leaders
- provide ongoing support for young leaders to deal with mistakes and upsets.

Creating opportunities for young people to practise their skills

In the Leadership Workshop young people are invited to turn inward, to investigate themselves, their relationships to others, and their thoughts, feelings and actions. They have examined their past and how it informs their present and their vision of the future. They have become aware of how they became trapped in a vicious circle, and have identified strategies and practised new skills to develop an alternative vision for who they are and who they can be in the world.

The next stage of the programme is very different. Here, they practise their new skills and understandings by turning outward, and begin the process of integrating their learning into their everyday lives.

The insights and skills they have gained in the training need to be put into practise quickly. Our experience shows that if there is a long gap between the Leadership Workshop and the next phase of development, then momentum can be lost and young people may slip back into old habits and old ways of seeing the world.

The facilitation team will have observed participants during the workshop and, with other staff, will have formed an assessment about individuals and the appropriate next steps. The project manager should work closely with the facilitation team and the individual participants at this stage to identify, plan and schedule these next steps and appropriate progression routes.

We suggest making different progression routes available for young people who have completed the Leadership Workshop, according to how profound their shift in attitudes and behaviours has been during the workshop. At this stage it is essential that young people are not set up to fail by being asked to take on challenges or roles that are too much of a reach for them. At the same time, young people who are ready need the opportunity to stretch and progress, and practise their new understanding and skills.

Some may need to complete the workshop a second time, to deepen their skills and self-awareness, and this should be communicated to the young person as a positive step. They should be encouraged to increase their level of participation and involvement in the workshop and to act as peer support and role models for young people attending the programme for the first time.

Some young people will be ready to go on to the other workshops described in Part 2 of this guidebook. The Advanced Leadership Workshop invites young people to deepen their self-awareness and application of leadership and conflict skills, and is ideal for individuals who have already acted as a mentor and leader for others in the programme.

The 'Fear and Fashion' Workshop explores the whole issue of carrying and using knives and can be used as a development of the Leadership Workshop, and a preparation for young people who want to create more awareness about this issue in their local community. The Leadership in Action workshop prepares young people to facilitate and lead others in group discussions and meetings. Leap also runs progression courses, where young people learn how to facilitate a session on leadership and conflict with other young people, or train to become peer mediators, helping others to manage and resolve conflict. All of these workshops prepare young people to take a step up into a leadership role where they *demonstrate* and role-model their new understanding and skills to other young people. This peer training cascade model is at the heart of Leap's approach to transformative programmes for young people. It can be summed up as 'learning from those above us by being alongside them'. It is also known as the 'ladder model'.

By encouraging participants to take up a leadership role with other young people, we let them know that we believe in them and are willing to invest in them. Practising a new way of being in the world opens up alternative ways of thinking, feeling and acting that become part of their everyday behaviour. By becoming peer leaders, they develop personal and emotional resilience, gain approval and affirmation from adults, and respect and admiration from their friends and peer groups. This starts them on a journey towards a different destination, back into education, training, employment, a respected place amongst their peers and families, and a sense of contributing to the wider community. Young people begin to believe that they matter, and this is reflected back to them by the community of support developed around the programme.

Using existing structures and activities

The roles that are made available to the participants need to be real and meaningful, and to have points of progression built into them. In this way young people gain a sense of direction and purpose: they can see the way ahead and what might be achieved. These roles should be supported either by the facilitation team or by other local staff in the partnership who have experienced the Leadership Workshops and can coach the young leaders in this stage of the programme.

We recommend identifying existing opportunities for young people, rather than trying to create a whole new context for them to practise their new skills. Young leaders can, for example, start off in small teams to deliver short workshops on conflict awareness and skills training to groups of students in schools, colleges, and youth centres. Most youth organisations will warmly welcome this peer education as a way to enrich their own programmes.

Planning for this should ensure that delivery opportunities provide enough of a challenge for the young leaders as they grow in confidence and skills. Factors such as the age of the participants they are training and group size will be important. In our experience it is better to start young leaders off in situations where they work in supportive teams, training younger people in small groups. As they progress in skills and confidence you can put them in more challenging situations. As the confidence of young leaders in the Leap 'Fear and Fashion' programme grew, for example, they began to deliver workshops to adults as part of a national anti-knife crime campaign, and gave presentations at conferences.

It is important to treat the young leaders professionally and seriously. Structured and supported planning time should be scheduled before they deliver a session, and afterwards they should debrief with an experienced staff member on what went well and what they would improve for next time. They need to be held accountable for their punctuality, reliability, professionalism and leadership of others. In this way they are encouraged to take responsibility for themselves and to take their own development seriously.

Onward progression routes

As young leaders gain opportunities to practise and develop their new skills and behaviour, they grow in confidence. However, there are still many dangers for them out there in the community in which they have grown up. Friends and family may be jealous of their new-found confidence, and their circumstances may be such that they are still vulnerable to temptation and peer pressure, particularly if their circumstances change, for example if a friend is attacked, they lose their girlfriend, etc. It is important to identify new challenges and onward progression routes for them, into education, training, voluntary work, or employment.

Many young people at risk dropped out of education early, either because they were excluded from mainstream education, or through truanting and non-attendance. Many find formal learning situations a challenge and they may have poor literacy and numeracy skills. Learning to manage conflict constructively and effectively and developing the skills of self-leadership to take responsibility for your own words and actions are important and valid competencies in their own right. The Leadership Programme can be delivered as an accredited programme, so that young people can have their learning validated. This can be an important first step back into training or education.

For many young people who come through the Leadership Programme, the Leadership Certificate is the first formal recognition of learning that they have ever received. Certificate ceremonies recognise and affirm their achievements and are part of the creation of a wider community of support around the programme. (See Chapter 5.)

In the Leap 'Fear and Fashion' programme, young people who graduated from the programme had the opportunity to apply for apprentice youth work roles within Westminster Young People's Services. They were also paid for delivering sessions to youth clubs in the local area. Other young people in the programme applied to join Leap's pool of young trainers.

The more a young person invests in a new vision for their future, the more they have to lose if they step back into their old ways of being. Other young people see the young leaders as role models, and begin to believe in the possibility of change for themselves. Where the young leaders were once admired for their talent to destroy, they are now admired because they are forging a different path for themselves and the young people who will come after them.

Providing ongoing support for young leaders to deal with mistakes and upsets

At this stage of their journey young people may still be vulnerable to relapse into old habits, and it is almost inevitable that they will make a mistake of some kind after the workshop. It is important that staff and partners plan for this. Your response will depend on the specifics of the incident, the previous history of the participant, and how serious the breakdown in behaviour is. Rather than seeing it as a reason to exclude the youth, or as a sign that the programme has failed, it may be helpful to put the incident into the context of the broader aims and values of the programme and see it as part of the learning process.

If young people do relapse, we recommend dealing with this within the concepts and values of the programme. One example is the process in the Leadership in Action workshop called 'Support Yourself' (see pages 152–154). The individual should be encouraged to own their mistake, acknowledge it with the parties concerned, and do what is necessary to repair any harm that has been done. Minor slip-ups and mistakes can be seen as opportunities for young leaders to practise the skills of taking responsibility and recommitting to the personal goals they defined for themselves during the Leadership Workshop.

In addition, young leaders may come under increased pressure from friends and family to revert to their old ways of behaving. Their peer group may feel jealous and threatened by the change in them. This can be a tough challenge for the young person and will need careful handling and support from the facilitators and partner agencies. One way of tackling this is to recruit the peer group onto a Leadership Workshop, so that they get to experience it for themselves. Providing plenty of opportunities for the young leader to demonstrate their skills, and making them feel part of a new and growing community of support, will also help. Through participating in the workshops they will have begun to develop a new group of friends and peers, and partner agencies and the local community can do much to strengthen the friendship bonds of this group by providing them with opportunities to take part in social activities and events together.

Young people often become more assertive after attending an effective programme. They start to express themselves clearly and make requests. This can disconcert some staff members, who may find this behaviour threatening and difficult to manage. In one prison, for example, more young inmates appeared in front of the governor *after* the programme's implementation. This was because they discussed issues with staff in a more assertive manner, which some staff saw as insubordination and disrespect. The increase in governors' reports could be seen as a deterioration, but the governor welcomed the change. He pointed out that assaults by young people on staff, as well as on each other, had fallen since implementation of the programme.

Some local partner staff will need training and support to handle and accept positive changes in behaviour, particularly if running the programme in a secure setting. It is a huge challenge for a staff member, as well as a young person, to take a new kind of relationship created within a safe workshop situation back into the general prison environment. Both staff and youth need guidance on how to handle this shift in relationship constructively. Sometimes a more open and honest relationship between staff and youth can be seen as an opportunity for one to take advantage of another, and the situation needs to be sensitively monitored.

Showing it works – tracking and proving the transformation

A programme is at its most vulnerable during its initial months, when it needs to prove itself to its supporters as well as critics. Partners and programme facilitators should not allow themselves to be disheartened by setbacks, or by expectations of immediate results. This can be pre-empted by the development and communication of clear programme expectations.

If you do not define and then communicate your short-term expectations, others will do it for you, making their own judgements on whether the programme is working or not. Their criteria might be based on their own agenda and bear no relation to the programme's stated intentions, but their criticism will carry weight if it is not balanced against your own clearly defined criteria. The gap between the programme's delivery and its results can be a very stressful time, and those involved in the programme can feel vulnerable.

We need to demonstrate that the programme works right from the start. We should not claim that 'We've got it all right and are producing all the results.' Rather, we should show that the programme is working well for that particular stage of the journey and process. This requires well thought-out targets and achievements for each session, each day, and each phase of the programme. We need to build criteria around what we said we would achieve using the cornerstones, foundations, etc.

In implementing the Leadership Programme in Feltham Young Offenders Institute, the team worked out a way to evaluate the weekly community meetings held on the unit, right from the start. They decided, for example, to monitor many of the targets they had set themselves by asking questions such as:

- How many young men chose to attend the meeting?
- How many young men actually spoke at the meeting?
- What range of issues was proposed for discussion?
- How many have we been able to deal with?
- How many young men took an active part in small group discussions?
- How many decisions were reached?

- How many decisions from the last meeting were put into practice?
- How many young men participated for the full meeting?
- How many young men took leadership roles in the meeting?
- How many times did participants interrupt each other?

These statistics enabled the team to monitor their progress from week to week. They also had something solid to share and discuss with others. They did not adopt a 'wait and see' attitude, but went on the offensive to nurture their dream, so that it could exist long enough for the programme to take hold, and for wider results to begin to show.

Extensive evaluation and monitoring criteria can be defined for a multi-purpose programme. These should be developed before delivery of the programme, so that everybody is clear on what and how information will be gathered. The gathering of baseline data against which to measure progress is supported through the initial conflict audit described in Chapter 2 (see page 28).

This process of constant monitoring and checking lies at the heart of the programme's ongoing development.

- *Participants* need to demonstrate to themselves that things are working and that their efforts are worthwhile.
- *Staff* need to demonstrate to themselves that they are on the right track.
- *Management* need to motivate the continuation of the programme.
- *Funders* need to know that their resources are being well used.
- *Policymakers* need to be encouraged by the results.

The demonstration of results is critical to all those involved in the process. Successes and achievements need to be constantly highlighted and affirmed, and mistakes and failures need to be acknowledged and constantly addressed. The Leadership Programme could be described as a process of demonstration, a 'walk the talk, do as I do' programme.

> *It is no use walking anywhere to preach unless our walking is our preaching.*
> *St Francis of Assissi*

Chapter 5

Gathering a Community of Support

There is no limit to what people can achieve,
As long as they don't care who gets the credit.

Bob Woodruff

Transformative programmes have the power to alter the way young people see themselves and perceive the world about them – and so fundamentally alter the course of their lives. Many young people are trapped in cycles of violence and challenging behaviour, linked to territorialism, gang loyalty, family feuds or peer pressure, and lead lives defined by cynicism and despair.

Transformative approaches recognise these lifestyles and behaviours as the outcome of complex and often deep-rooted personal, social or family factors, often multi-layered and with hidden influences and sources. Transformative programmes aim to help participants untangle some of this underlying complexity. Initially, they provide resources for the individuals – skills, self-awareness, confidence and self-responsibility. In the next stage young people can practise and increase their resources and build resilience for future challenges in their own lives. Programme graduates adopt roles in which they cascade their learning to others and contribute to their communities, schools and estates. Transformative programmes seize the opportunity to engage with a broader context and to meet the underlying issues with responses that are equally broad and embracing.

Gathering a community of support around the programme is a process that begins in the first phases of programme design and continues throughout the life of the programme. This is about developing, disseminating and developing further:

- developing a community of support – the structures that supports the programme
- disseminating and continuing to develop.

Developing a community of support – the structures that support the programme

During the initial engagement period the following need to be focused on:

- engaging with partners
- agreeing project structure and management
- roles and responsibilities
- written agreements.

Engaging with partners

Leap's experience is that successful transformative programmes are partnership programmes where agencies, organisations and individuals work together to develop and deliver the programme, with each partner working to their strengths and contributing to agreed shared aims. We know that working with partners can be more challenging than working alone. Issues of power, of resources, and of different organisational cultures and agendas are inherent in most partnerships, but the benefits nearly always outweigh the costs. Years of experience at Leap tell us that no one agency or organisation can provide all the resources that the young people will need for support as they break out of destructive cycles of behaviour.

Key partners may include:

- professional agencies and organisations, including:
  - the police
  - Youth Offending Teams
  - the education service
  - the Youth Service
  - community and mental health service
  - colleges and schools
  - local voluntary organisations and services
  - young offender institutions
  - local authorities
- young people
- local area community organisations, such as:
  - residents/tenants associations
  - mediation service
- funders
- a single institution, such as a school or a prison.

Agreeing project structure and management

Initial meetings and discussions are likely to be held with strategic and policy leads from different local agencies. However, as the programme moves into delivery mode, it is more useful to involve operational staff in the regular local partnership meetings. As long as they have the support of senior managers, they are more likely to have time to resource the programme properly, and will have the local knowledge and contacts that can make things happen. Strategic meetings can be scheduled at relevant milestones as a vehicle for review and performance monitoring.

Different agencies and organisations have different organisational cultures and procedures to follow. It is useful to discuss these early on, so that each partner understands the decision-making processes and powers of the different representatives.

The following could also be discussed:

- How often will meetings happen?
- Who will circulate agendas, chair meetings and take notes?
- How will the progress of the programme be monitored, evaluated and reviewed?

- What channels of communication will be used?
- How will success be defined and measured?
- How will the successes of the programme be communicated, and by whom?
- How will the partnership be described to others?
- Are there any ownership or branding issues that need to be agreed?

Roles and responsibilities

It is important to be clear what each partner contributes to the programme. It could be practical resources such as a venue, equipment, transport, local networks, funds, staff, specialist expertise, etc. Different partners can commit to different responsibilities, such as: referring individual young people; providing local intelligence and knowledge; organising delivery opportunities for young leaders; carrying out risk assessments and dealing with safeguarding issues; and local promotion of the programme.

Written agreements

It is good to capture these partnership discussions in a written agreement, and to consider together what will happen if there is a disagreement or a breakdown in communication, or a partner reneges on a responsibility or commitment, for example cancelling a workshop at the last minute.

It is almost inevitable that there will be differences of opinion, obstacles, and areas of disagreement over the life of a programme. Having a written agreement, which includes a clear dispute resolution strategy that is shared and agreed by all partners, means that there is a structure and process in place to deal with any differences that occur.

Disseminating and continuing to develop

- Celebrating achievement
- Developing support staff
- Holding the hope

As the programme begins to achieve tangible results it is important to *disseminate* the good work and to continue *developing* the programme. This begins to widen the community of support around the programme, beyond the local partnership and into the community, involving parents, schools, politicians, other agencies and community members. Spreading the word is infectious. Sharing good results inspires others, and builds confidence and self-belief in all those involved. When we can clearly articulate the way things are working it helps to motivate us. Being open about, and addressing, what is not working means that the partnership takes the initiative, rather than waiting for someone else to point out the problem.

By disseminating the results of our work we promote generosity; encouraging others to share their ideas, knowledge and skills and get involved. This can result in new opportunities for the young leaders to practise their skills and become ambassadors for the programme. As the recipients of the programme they become the most effective disseminators of the work, and they recruit the next cohorts of young people.

Celebrating achievement

It is important to find ways to affirm the achievements of the young leaders in public so that they are witnessed by the wider community around the programme.

In the 'Fear and Fashion' programme, Leap and the local partnership ran regular certificate ceremonies to celebrate these achievements. Parents and carers, siblings, staff and management from the different partner agencies, the wider Leap team, local dignitaries and funders were invited to take part in a workshop run by the young leaders, followed by a certificate ceremony. On occasion, the chair of the advisory board for the funding consortium, a local QC, presented the certificates – the first time that many of the young people had a positive reason to stand in front of a barrister! In closing the ceremony, many of the young people would comment on what it meant to them to have a group of adults listen to them, and be there to celebrate their achievement.

In the prison, the Number 1 Governor (the head of the prison) always attended the last half-hour of the Leadership Workshops to affirm the young men's achievement and to present them with certificates.

Developing support staff

Staff from the partner agencies have a crucial part to play in the delivery of the programme. They help recruit participants, publicise and communicate the work to the wider community, and offer individual young people one-to-one support. While the Leap team provides the specialist input and training for the young people, the support staff provide day-to-day ongoing coaching and mentoring for individual participants. They know the local area and how best to create opportunities for the young leaders to practise their skills. Without them, it would be impossible to deliver the programme effectively.

These staff can be encouraged and supported to learn some of the key understandings and skills for working with conflict for themselves, so that they are better able to support young people undertaking the programme. In the prison programmes, for example, Leap offers training to key staff in youth and conflict skills, with the aim that prison officers will eventually deliver the programme, supported by the Leap team.

Support staff are also encouraged to attend the Leadership Workshops with the young people, so that they get to know the materials and techniques and can refer to particular skills or concepts when they work with young people at a later stage. The workshops also give them an opportunity to develop a different kind of relationship with participants. If staff feel comfortable enough to share some aspects of themselves, young people get to see that adults also face challenges, get hooked into conflicts, and may also find it hard to manage their feelings.

In the closing rounds of the workshops young people would often comment on the new appreciation they had for staff, and their own new awareness that there are some things that we all have in common as human beings. In the prison workshops, inmates referred regularly to 'seeing behind the uniform' and how important that had been for them. These new relationships continued back on the wing, and both officers and inmates could refer back to their shared learning from the workshop when dealing with challenging or difficult situations that might arise in the future.

Holding the hope

Transformative programmes turn despair into hope. The hope of change and positive transformation for the young people and for their community is the unifying force that holds the various elements of the programme together like strong glue.

Transformation can only happen if a community of support has been built. This community comes to understand the transformation process over the life of the programme, and each partner values the vital contribution that they make, and that others make, to each stage and aspect of the programme. Partners learn to negotiate and overcome challenges and obstacles with good grace, giving attention to the needs and contributions of fellow partners, agencies and professionals. Just as the young person embarks on a journey at the beginning of the programme, so too do the partners and stakeholders, until there is a whole host of adults 'holding the hope' for young people until they are able to hold it for themselves, and for other young people in their community.

I have to cast my lot with those who age after age, perversely,
With no extraordinary power, reconstitute the world.

Adrienne Rich

Part II

The Leadership Programme

Notes for Facilitators

These materials are designed with experienced and skilled facilitators in mind, and we would strongly recommend that you undertake training and development in facilitating group work with challenging young people before you take on delivering this work.

Participants will challenge and inspire you, and take you to your learning edge. You will need to pay careful attention to team preparation and planning, and you may require external supervision to support you as a team and help you develop your practice. We suggest you read Part 1 of this guidebook to familiarise yourself with the wider aims, values and underpinning philosophy of the Leadership Programme as a starting point for preparing to deliver the workshops.

These materials have been designed for use with young people aged 16 and over. They would need to be adapted and tailored for use with a younger age range, by making sessions shorter and adjusting the focus of some of the exercises. Central themes running through the Leadership Programme are those of 'choice' and 'taking responsibility'. However, it is important to recognise some of the constraints young people may be under in exercising self-leadership. Facilitators should be sensitive to external factors outside the young person's control which may impact on the range of choices available to them, for example, community, family and cultural factors.

The facilitators' main function is to create the space and environment in which learning and personal discovery can occur for the participants. All we are doing is providing the young people with an opportunity so that they can do it for themselves. Participants will be looking to the facilitators to set the tone and atmosphere of workshops.

Facilitators can use every moment, whatever it is, to create a learning opportunity. You can use moments that are challenging, emotional, sad, happy, funny, insulting or intense. You can use moments of pain, of anger, of fear, of warmth; or moments of interest, of boredom, of despair, of optimism. Any one of these can provide you, as well as the group, with a learning experience. So the motto is, *use everything that happens as an opportunity for growth.*

The workshops

Each workshop is preceded by an introduction which outlines the overall aim and the focus of each day. The introduction also covers any particular information which is necessary in order to support successful delivery. For example, the Advanced Leadership Workshop introduction explores the concept of 'Acts'; the 'Fear and Fashion' Workshop examines some of the context within which young people carry and use knives. The Leadership and Advanced Leadership Workshops are more internally focused; they represent the 'turning inwards' that young people need to do in order to truly understand how they can begin to exercise and demonstrate self-leadership. The Leadership in Action and 'Fear and Fashion' Workshops are more externally focused, representing the 'turning out' that young people do as part of practising and demonstrating their new skills back in their communities.

It is better if facilitators work in teams of two or three, never on their own. This provides for:

- a variety of presentation styles
- facilitators supporting each other, so that one facilitator does not have to run the whole show
- sharing experience
- extra support for the young people
- a facilitator in each small group when the participants divide up.

Experienced facilitators, familiar with the particular techniques used in this workshop, will be able to adapt these materials and make them their own very quickly. However, we would recommend that those with less experience in this style of group work allow themselves time to develop.

First, try to assimilate the materials. This is best done by facilitating and gaining practice and confidence. (For most people this is a big enough challenge to start with.)

Second, try to put yourself into the materials, by colouring them with your stories, your examples, with your life experience and your personality. This process will really bring the work to life.

Once you have accomplished this, then you are ready to embark on re-creating this work in your own way. This is all part of a creative and developmental process.

Make sure that the facilitation team has enough time beforehand for team-building, planning and preparation. It is a good idea to run an exercise with each other if you need clarity. It is also vital to the performance of the team to build in time at the end of each day to reflect on the work, on the level of participation, and on your facilitation.

There is a risk involved in this work. However, the risk in this context is not one of damage, but of the unknown. If our fear of the unpredictable is very strong, it could lead us to become overprotective of the participants and, therefore, limit their learning opportunities.

Some useful guidelines

- **Create boundaries:** for acceptable behaviour, timekeeping, punctuality, staying unhooked. Create a safe and conducive environment for you and the participants.
- **Expect the unexpected:** so that when it happens you are ready for it and can welcome it. Accept and work with expressions of feelings and emotions, be they distress or aggression.
- **Respond to actions and situations without taking them personally:** if you take things personally it will make you less effective as a facilitator. Your job is to create a safe and supportive learning environment and encourage full participation. Enable participants to follow a process and to take responsibility for their own emotions and feelings.
- **Make use of your experience:** share your own successes and failures without judgement or advice, simply as another person who has a story to tell. Participants will relate to whatever is meaningful to them.
- **Acknowledge your own feelings:** most important of all, to yourself, and then to your colleagues, and finally, if appropriate, to the young people. Don't pretend all is well when it is not. Seek out support from your colleagues. We must practice in our lives what we would like the participants to apply in their lives. However, always remember that this is about the young people, the participants and not yourself. Only use carefully edited

examples of your own experiences and feelings if it will help the journey of the young people.

- **Remember that values are 'caught, not taught':** participants absorb and develop values by experiencing them in practice. They learn from the facilitators who practise the values themselves.

- **Facilitators are also on the course:** it is essential that the facilitators live the programme and do not merely facilitate it. They need constantly to check how well they are taking a lead in their own lives.

Presenting a workshop

It is important that facilitators find interesting and varied ways of presenting the material to maintain the interest and engagement of participants. Here are some examples of successful ways in which people have chosen to present various sections of a workshop.

Introducing the theme of a workshop

One facilitator used graphics and storytelling when introducing the theme of taking a lead in life. She drew a picture of a large mountain and told a story of a mountain climber, using the mountain as a metaphor for personal leadership. She created the picture of the climber trying out different methods to get to the top. It was an entertaining, stimulating and creative way to get the participants involved in the content of the workshop right from the start.

Introducing the focus of each day

One facilitator used props when explaining the relationship between the past, the present, and the future in the Leadership Workshop. The past was represented by a large cardboard box full of experiences. The present was represented by a handbag full of objects like keys, money and jewellery. The future was represented by a large sheet of clean paper. These props were laid down on the floor in a straight line and were moved around according to the responses of the group.

For example, when asked the question 'Are we actually present in the present?' a participant replied, 'No, the past is always with us.' The facilitator then moved the box and placed it over the handbag so that it could not be seen any more. This made the presentation dramatic. When asked 'If this is what the present looks like, then what would the future look like?' one participant lifted the box with the handbag still inside, and placed them on top of the large sheet of paper. This was a powerful physical image that would not easily be forgotten by those in the workshop.

Another facilitator asked a volunteer to stand up in front of the group. He represented someone in the present. A jacket represented his past experience. The facilitator threw the jacket over the participant's head so that the participants couldn't see him and he couldn't see them. It was a memorable image. People laughed at the picture it created and the image stimulated active discussion and debate.

Introducing the workshop games and exercises

All of the examples given above – the graphics, metaphors, storytelling, props, dramatic presentation, physical images and pictures – can be used to introduce any aspect of the workshops. Facilitators have also used role-play – taking on the role and speech of a character to introduce a behaviour or attitude that will be explored in an exercise. They have also used physical movements and body positions to demonstrate a type of reaction in certain situations.

Exercises

A short description of each exercise is given, followed by instructions for how to lead it. Discussion questions are suggested in the 'Feedback' section, and there is a detailed comment section for each exercise, giving guidance on facilitation.

There are several feedback sessions in a workshop day. It is crucial that the pace, style and intensity of each feedback is varied, in order to sustain interest. You should use your initiative according to the participants' energy levels, concentrations spans, and what happened in the course of a particular exercise. The questions indicated are purely suggestions to help you maintain a focus throughout the day. You can devise your own. Feedback could sometimes occur in pairs or in small groups. Feedback could be led with a series of questions, or could be just a brief check to see what people might want to say about the previous exercise before moving on.

You should not feel obliged to debrief every exercise. You might feel the participants need a 'rest' and that a thorough debrief is not necessary on every occasion. Sometimes just the experience of participating in an exercise is enough. Again it is a question of keeping a balance between participating, experiencing and reflecting.

Debriefs

We strongly recommend that the facilitation team debrief thoroughly with key workers and support staff at the end of each day of the workshop, and, if possible, that you have quick check-in breaks between sessions. These debriefs and check-ins are vital for assessing how the workshop is going, developing strategies for dealing with any challenging behaviour or emerging tensions, and ensuring that you are achieving the aims and objectives of the workshop. Any participation issues and/or concerns emerging about individual participants can be shared with the team and strategies put in place to address them. For example, if a particular participant appears to be struggling, you may create an opportunity for a facilitator or support worker to talk to them privately.

For more guidance on facilitating this work see *Playing with Fire* (Macbeth and Fine 2011).

Chapter 6
The Leadership Workshop

Introduction to the Leadership Workshop

This workshop is the first in a comprehensive programme designed to make a positive impact on a community or a specific institution. Young people can graduate from this workshop to the Advanced Leadership, Leadership in Action and 'Fear and Fashion' Workshops, depending on the overall aims and objectives of the programme. Although the Leadership Workshop has some impact when experienced on its own, it is far more effective when experienced as part of a transformative programme for young people.

The workshop works best when delivered as a block, rather than in weekly sessions. In this version of the Leadership Workshop six hours are needed each day (consisting of two three-hour sessions). This does not include short breaks and meal breaks. However, in community programmes young people may be unable to commit to a whole day, and the material can be reorganised to suit different settings, according to the needs of the group.

The workshop focus

This workshop focuses on personal leadership. The aim is aligned to the overarching aim of the Leadership Programme as a whole: to develop the leadership potential within every participant so that they become contributing members of their communities.

The vision statement, foundations, cornerstones, building blocks and statements on leadership can all be used to introduce the focus of the workshop on the first day. We also begin with the key question: 'If you want to be a leader, who is the first person you need to lead?'

This workshop takes participants on a journey of six stages:

1. Taking Stock

2. Unpacking the Punch

3. Cracking the Act

4. Breaking Out

5. Taking a Stand

6. Moving On.

The journey takes the participants from the present to the past to the future. Day 1 focuses on the present, Day 2 looks at the influence of the past, and on Day 3 we focus on building a future.

INTRODUCE THE WORKSHOP THEME

It is important to highlight the leadership theme in the introduction. Facilitators could share their own experience of the workshop with participants, as well as a personal story related to taking leadership in their own lives. This encourages the young people to relate to the content, creates a relationship between them and the facilitators, and sets the tone for the workshop.

EXPLAIN THE ACTIVITIES

Tell the participants about the various activities – for example, listening, speaking and thinking; sitting, standing, walking and running; discussing and contributing their ideas; being challenged and supported; taking part in exercises and games.

OUTLINE YOUR ROLE

It would be useful to say something along the following lines: 'We are not teachers, we are not preachers, we do not have all the answers, we are not here to tell you how to live your life, to give you solutions, or to make choices for you. The answers lie within you. It is up to you to find your own answers, your own solutions, to make your own choices. We are here to facilitate this workshop, to explain the exercises, to encourage participation, to maintain the focus, to help with timekeeping, to assist with the learning process, and to provide support where necessary.'

OUTLINE THE ROLE OF THE PARTICIPANTS

A possible line to take would be: 'What you get out of this workshop is entirely up to you. What you put in you will get out. We would encourage you to try everything, even if you feel a bit strange or awkward, you feel a bit scared or shy, you feel you don't want to make a fool of yourself. Your participation will help others to have a go. By taking the lead in participating, you will help yourself as well as others. Work hard at listening, even if you disagree with what is being said: you might learn something. If you have something to say, say it, don't hold back, because others might learn from you. So go for it and you will get an enormous amount out of it.'

Workshop guidelines

We recommend using predetermined guidelines. At the Advanced Leadership Workshop you could review these guidelines and negotiate them with participants. At this early stage, however, it is enough of a challenge for the group to observe the guidelines suggested below.

- Allow everyone to finish what they are saying.
- Only one speaker at a time – no interruptions.
- Support and encourage each other – no put-downs, verbal or physical abuse, no distractions.
- Volunteer yourself only – allow others to make their own choices. You have the right to pass.
- Observe confidentiality – show respect for others. What is said here, stays here.
- Mobile phones to be switched off during sessions.

You could add other guidelines that are specific to your context and the young people attending.

PRACTICAL ISSUES AND HOUSEKEEPING

Share all relevant information with the group. The policy on attendance and on who will be eligible for a certificate needs to be clear from the start.

Day 1

Focus: *On the present*

Taking stock – unpacking the punch

Agenda

Session 1

- Introduction to the Workshop
- Personal Introductions
- The Big Wind Blows On
- Leadership Wordstorm
- Focus of the Day
- Personal Qualities
- Grandma's Keys
- My Life
- Trust Circle Walk

Session 2

- Bombs and Shields
- Red Rags
- Getting Hooked
- Closing

Quotes to Introduce the Day

For news of the heart, ask the face.
from Guinea

You can't shake hands with a clenched fist.
Indira Ghandi

You don't have to turn around and look at every dog that barks at you.
from Haiti

Most powerful are those who have themselves in their own power.
Seneca

Session 1

Introduction to the workshop

Facilitators cover the following points (referring to the section 'Introduction to the Leadership Workshop, on pages 57–58).

- The workshop theme – how to take a lead in life.
- What participants will do in the workshop.
- The role of the facilitators.
- How to get the most out of the workshop.
- Workshop guidelines.
- Practical issues and housekeeping – times, breaks, meals, attendance, certificates, etc.

Personal Introductions – an introductory group exercise

Go round the group, and give each participant a chance to answer the question 'What is your name and why have you chosen to attend this workshop?'

COMMENTS

Encourage participants to think for themselves. Do not allow them merely to copy each other by repeating what the last person said (for example, 'I came to the workshop because I am bored,' or 'I don't know why I came, I just decided to come'). Allow one or two to copy, and then intervene. Explore with them possible reasons they had for deciding to attend. These choices lie at the heart of the workshop, and must go beyond 'I came because I was told to come'. It is important to create this atmosphere right at the start, but make sure to do so in a friendly, non-threatening way.

The Big Wind Blows On/The Sun Shines On/The Rain Falls On – an icebreaker

The title you choose for this game depends on the day's weather.

You will need one less chair than there are players. Chairs should be arranged in a circle. Ask for a volunteer to stand in the centre of the circle. One participant stands in the centre of the circle and says something true about themselves, beginning with 'The Big Wind blows on anyone who…'

If what they say is also true for anyone sitting down, then those people have to move to another chair. The person in the middle goes to sit down on an empty chair, and a new person will be left standing in the middle.

You may want to add some rules, such as 'You can't return to the chair you have just come from, or go to a chair on either side of it. You have to cross the circle.'

In this game the participants start to share themselves and get to know one another a little better. The participant in the centre of the circle can start off with things that can be seen, such as: 'The Sun shines on all those wearing jeans'. The facilitator then moves the game on to things that can't be seen, such as: 'The Sun shines on all those with an elder brother', and then on to issues around leadership and conflict, such as: 'The Sun shines on all those who have been in a fight with someone'.

COMMENTS

This exercise is useful for the facilitators, as it starts to reveal the issues that are relevant to the group, and their common experiences. It can also show the participants that they are not necessarily alone in their experiences, and that this workshop can be a place for them to share those experiences. They see what they have in common with the facilitators, and that difficult subjects are not necessarily taboo.

Questions that come from the centre of the circle often refer to someone's fears, dislikes or regrets.

Every exercise in this workshop provides an opportunity to create an atmosphere that encourages sharing, whether it be through intimacy, attentive listening, humour, fun, relaxation or being challenged.

Leadership Wordstorm – a large-group exercise

Participants call out their responses to the questions:

- What do we mean by leadership?
- What is leadership?

And then:

- What do we mean by personal leadership or self-leadership?
- What does it mean to lead yourself?

The facilitators write the responses up on a large sheet of paper.

Participants are then asked to call out their responses to another question:

- What qualities and skills do you need in order to lead yourself?

Note: Before participants respond to this question, the facilitators ask them to explain what a skill is, and what a quality is. *For example*: a skill is the ability to do something, a quality is a way of being, a way of behaving. The facilitators get clarity on the meaning of these words by getting participants to give specific examples. They then return to the question above and write the participants' responses up on a second large sheet of paper.

COMMENTS

This exercise helps facilitators to engage with the participants. It is a gentle way of introducing the workshop theme and intention to the group. It begins to acknowledge who we are, what skills and qualities we have, what skills we feel are missing, and the qualities we would like to develop. It begins to create space for the participants to pause and reflect.

Focus of the Day

On the present: Taking stock – unpacking the punch

On Day 1 participants carry out a personal check on themselves at that point in time. They begin to think about who they are, the qualities they have, the qualities they would like to have, what upsets them, how they do things, how they think about things and how they react to pressure.

Discuss the focus with the participants, linking it to the Leadership Wordstorm and to the next exercise.

You could use the quotes on page 60 to encourage a discussion on the Focus of the Day.

See Notes for Facilitators: 'Presenting a workshop' and 'Introducing the focus of each day' on page 55.

Personal Qualities – a large-group sharing exercise

Ask the participants, first, to choose from the leadership wordstorm one quality/skill which they feel they already have, and then a second that they feel they would like to develop. Ask them to share these with the group.

Write their responses up next to their names on a large sheet of paper. Participants will now be expected to demonstrate the first quality/skill during the workshop, and to start demonstrating the second quality/skill immediately. Now that this is 'public', they can receive feedback and support from the rest of the group during the workshop.

Comments

This public declaration by participants of their own qualities and skills, and of their intention to develop further, begins a process of community building, affirmation and support. You can only support someone when they are clear about what they want to achieve and commit themselves to achieving it. It is vital that such information is shared with others, so that they can hold us accountable, and we can allow them to support us. The process of asking for and giving support starts early in the workshop.

The facilitators might ask participants if they are willing to receive feedback and support in order to help them to develop the skill and/or quality they have identified.

You can bring participants back to this list at various points in the workshop. *For example*: you could ask them to reflect silently on how they are doing. You could ask them to acknowledge someone else for an achievement within the workshop. Later in the process you could ask them to acknowledge themselves for something they have accomplished related to this exercise.

Facilitators can give individual participants feedback that begins very gently but becomes more rigorous as the workshop develops. For example: 'On the first morning you said that you were a great listener, but you don't seem to be demonstrating that quality in this group'.

Facilitators should participate in this exercise and give examples of their own skills and qualities. This emphasises that we should all be involved in continual practice, improvement and application, and be open to feedback and support.

Grandma's/Grandpa's Keys – a team-building cooperative game

Choose one participant to be 'Grandma' (or 'Grandpa'). They stand at one end of the room, with their back to the rest of the group at the other end of the room. Grandma/Grandpa has a set of keys on the floor behind them. The group has to get to Grandma/Grandpa and take the keys back to the other end of the room. Every time Grandma/Grandpa turns round, they must freeze. Anyone seen moving is sent back to the start.

Once someone has the keys, Grandma/Grandpa has to guess who that person is. If their guess is correct, the keys are returned, and the person discovered is sent back to the start.

Whenever Grandma/Grandpa guesses incorrectly, he/she turns round and the game continues.

The keys must be passed from hand to hand and not thrown across the floor or through the air. Participants are encouraged to concentrate, focus and strategise.

Feedback

Facilitators lead a brief discussion to reflect on this group exercise. Possible questions to use are: 'What worked well in the group? What didn't work well? When did you decide to change your tactics? How were these changes made? What skills were used in this game? What qualities were being shown? Was it easy to participate? What made it easy/difficult? Was it easy to be part of the group?'

COMMENTS

Facilitators can encourage the quieter participants to give their responses. It is important to build an atmosphere in which everyone's views are valued and are listened to. Every exercise on Day 1 prepares the ground for deeper sharing during the rest of the workshop, and provides an opportunity for the participants to grow in confidence and to gain trust in the facilitators and each other.

My Life – a sharing exercise in pairs

Divide the participants into two equal groups. One group can sit on a close circle of chairs facing outwards, and the other group can sit in a wider circle of chairs facing inwards, so that each person has a partner sitting opposite them.

Each time a question is asked, one partner responds and the other partner just listens. They then swap over. Recommend that they just listen, don't interrupt, don't make a contribution, don't give their partner any advice, don't say anything. They should *just listen*, and see what it feels like.

Give clear instructions as to time and who starts, and get one circle to move round after each question is complete, so that participants work with at least four partners.

The questions are:

- Describe someone in your life whom you respect/admire/who inspires you/you've learnt from…and why

- Describe a time in your life when you felt proud about what you did…and why.

- Describe a time in your life when you didn't feel proud about what you did…and why.

- Describe a time in your life when you resolved a difficult situation without violence. What skills or qualities did you use?

- Describe a quality you would like your children/a child to see in you…and why.

Feedback

Facilitators lead a discussion about the exercise. Focus first on the questions that were asked. 'Which of the questions were easier to find a response to…and why? Which of the questions were tougher to find a response to…and why? Was there something that you said or remembered that surprised you? What was it? Was there something that someone else shared that surprised you? What was it?'

The feedback focus now shifts to listening and sharing. 'What was it like just to be listened to? What was it like to share with someone else? What was it like to listen to someone else? Was there anything that you noticed when listening or sharing, about yourself or your partner? What is important about listening? About being listened to? What is important about sharing yourself with others? About others sharing themselves with you? How often are you really listened to in your life?'

COMMENTS

This exercise is often difficult to facilitate. Participants can become restless, embarrassed, start to joke or to distract one another, etc. Most participants will find it uncomfortable to share themselves, especially with someone who just listens and does not interrupt. Most participants will find it unusual just to listen, without contributing.

The ability to sit still with someone else, to slow down, to be quiet, to relax, to be completely focused on what you are saying, to be part of what you are listening to, to give your full attention to somebody – these are skills and qualities that only develop with time and practice. So expect it to be tough, but don't reflect any possible concern in the way you introduce this exercise. Always expect the best from the participants. So speak in a way that shows them you know they can and will do it, however long it takes.

This is just the start of a long process. Quality communication – communication that includes both speaking and listening – forms the basis of any supportive community. For many of the participants it means moving from one model of communication to another.

This Leadership Workshop shifts continually from periods of dynamic activity to times of reflection, stillness, and sometimes silence. It is important to maintain this balance. With experience and practice the participants will become more comfortable with this, and create more space for themselves to reflect on their lives and their futures. They will create more opportunities to support each other by listening.

Trust Circle Walk – a group trust exercise

Ask a participant to stand in the middle of the circle with their eyes closed. They start walking. When the walker reaches the other participants in the circle, they gently redirect them in a new direction to cross the circle again.

The participants act as a protective wall. They create an atmosphere in which the walker can relax and trust that they will be well cared for. The circle can be made larger or smaller, depending on the confidence of the participant in the middle.

Facilitators encourage everyone to have a turn. This exercise is best done in silence. A further challenge to the group would be to have two participants walking in the circle at the same time.

Feedback

Possible questions to ask are: 'What was it like for you out there in the middle of the circle? What was it like for you to close your eyes and walk? What was it like for you to trust the group with your safety? What did it take for you to do this exercise? What was it like to be part of the circle, the protective wall? What was it like for you to be trusted by someone else? Do you trust people easily? Do people trust you easily? What does lack of trust *in* others cost you in life? What does lack of trust *from* others cost you?'

COMMENTS

Encourage every participant to take part. Ideally, everyone will do the full exercise and spend some time walking with their eyes closed in the circle. If someone is struggling, you could give them the option of doing the exercise with their eyes open. If a participant won't do that, you could give them the option of standing still in the centre of the circle with their eyes closed, or open, just to experience how it feels. If they will not step into the middle, you can still congratulate them on the support they give everyone else during the exercise. By being part of the wall, they make it possible for others to participate.

As facilitators we always need to focus on the specific achievements of the participants, to encourage them to take the next step for themselves. We need to remain flexible and creative in the way we engage with them. In this particular exercise, given their life experience, trusting others and allowing others to have physical contact with them, especially when they have their eyes closed and are feeling vulnerable, can be a huge challenge. Facilitators need to keep a balance between being sensitive to the needs of a participant and encouraging them to try something that is particularly tough.

Session 2

Bombs and Shields – a warm-up exercise in four parts

Everyone stands in a circle. Ask each participant to choose one other person in the group, without telling that person that they have been chosen. Explain to the group that their choice is not personal – they are choosing someone merely as a point of reference in the exercise.

Mark out the physical space in the room in which the exercise will take place. Explain to the participants that the person they have chosen is their 'bomb' – i.e. a threat to them – and that they must keep as far away from them as possible.

Facilitators call the start. Participants move around for a few seconds before the facilitator calls them to a stop.

The participants return to stand in a circle. Now they each choose another person in the group, again without saying who it is. This time, their chosen person is their 'shield', and protects them. During the exercise they must stay as close as possible to their shield, to be safe. Again, the facilitators start and end this part.

Now ask the participants to try to keep themselves as far as possible from their bomb, while keeping their shield between them and their bomb for protection. Again, the facilitators start and end this part.

For the final part, ask participants to keep themselves at all times at an equal distance from their 'bomb' and their 'shield' – for example, forming a triangle, with their 'bomb' and 'shield' as the other two points. Again, the facilitators call the start and end of this part.

Feedback

Facilitators lead a brief reflection on this warm-up exercise to introduce the theme for this session. Useful questions to ask are: 'What did it feel like avoiding your bomb all the time in the first part? Who had the control in that situation? Which person/people or which situations in your life does that remind you of? What was it like being so close to your shield all the time in the second part? Who had the control in that situation? Which people or which situations in your life does that remind you of? What was it like having to use the shield to protect you from the bomb in the third part? Who had control then? Who or what protects you in life like that? If the bomb was part of you, if it was inside you, what could it be? What was it like being at an equal distance from the two people in the final part? Who had control then? If that was a relationship you had with two people, what would it be like?'

Red Rags – a short role-play exercise

You might use this introduction to link 'Red Rags' to the previous exercise, along the following lines: 'Imagine the bomb was your own anger, your temper or your emotions, and could explode or burn inside you under particular circumstances. Imagine a situation in which you feel you lose control of yourself, you feel your emotions are controlling you. Someone says something to you or someone does something to you, and you react, you experience powerful emotions. This exercise is called Red Rags. It gets its name from the expression 'red rag to a bull' – when a red rag is waved in front of the bull, it 'sees red' and charges for it, as if out of control.'

Ask participants to choose a situation in which another person says or does something that would make them react in a violent, aggressive or abusive manner.

They rehearse this situation with a partner. They tell their partner what role they must play (for example, 'my father'), and explain what they should say – for example, 'You are too young to know what you're talking about!' The scene should only last a few seconds. It literally freezes that moment when hurt or anger is experienced. The partners then swap over. Each pair should have two short scenes to show the rest of the group, so that every participant has one turn.

Coordinate the pairs playing their scenes back. After each scene, ask the participant whose scene it was to give a one-word description of how it feels when that situation happens in real life – for example, 'insulting', 'humiliating', etc. Repeat all the descriptions that are given by the participants, and ask if the scenes have anything in common.

COMMENTS

Sometimes there is a need in the group, especially if it is a group of young men, to show some bravado. In their choice and their enactment of the short scenes they might want to show how 'bad' they are, how 'tough' they are, or how 'sharp/clever' they are. It is an opportunity to impress the rest of the group and the facilitators with the drama of their life experience. At this stage of the workshop it is a good idea to let them do their thing. It relaxes them, encourages participation, and, more often than not, everyone has a good laugh.

The freeze technique is useful in keeping the scenes short, and controls any violent incident or retaliation that is being portrayed.

Sometimes participants do not wish to demonstrate their scene in front of the whole group. In this case you could ask them just to talk through the incident.

It is important to keep the focus of all participants on the pair who are sharing their scenes at any given moment. This must be established on Day 1 and monitored throughout the workshop. Giving everyone the space to contribute, and appreciating their contribution, is vital for building trust and confidence in the process.

Getting Hooked – a structured role-play exercise

You might use this introduction to link 'Getting Hooked' to the previous exercise: 'Our purpose here is to take a look at what happens to people when they lose control of themselves in difficult or stressful situations. The red rag is like a hook that gets hold of us, so that we could say we actually get hooked, just like a fish. We lose all control and the person on the other end just reels us in. So we will look at what happens when we get hooked, at how the more hooked we get, the more our options are shut down, like going down an ever narrowing tunnel. If we can understand what happens to us at such times, then we can work on a way to get unhooked and to get back our control and power in challenging situations. Today, we will discover how the "bomb" of anger inside us is put together, and get to know its many parts. In a session tomorrow, we will look at how to defuse the bomb and take away its power over us. As an example, we will use a hook that regularly "catches" people: a verbal insult.'

As in 'Red Rags', this role-play exercise is very focused and brief. One participant plays the insulter, and the other plays the insulted person.

Choose one of the role-plays from the previous exercise, and ask the 'insulter' to stand at one end of the room, opposite the 'insulted' person. Place a line of four empty chairs between them.

The participants replay the scene: repeat the insult, and the reaction.

They then play the scene again, but this time the insulted person must 'have a thought' before they can react by saying something or approaching the insulter. Ask another participant to sit in the first empty chair, and the insulted person to stand next to that chair. The person sitting thinks of a thought that might be going through the insulted person's mind – the type of thought that would encourage them to get hooked into a confrontation with the insulter – and says this thought out loud.

A second participant comes to sit in the next chair, and utters another thought to 'wind up' or provoke the insulted person, who moves forward each time they are fed with a thought.

This is repeated with the third and fourth chairs. The series of chairs provides a train of thought that pushes the insulted person to react to the verbal abuse.

After seeing the first version, repeat the exercise, with other participants taking over the roles.

Once you have a variety of thoughts available, you can start to describe the different impact of each thought, such as a provoking thought, a justification, an excuse, a manipulating thought, a fearful thought, etc. The group can now start to 'unpack the punch' and distinguish the various stages of the hooking process, using the analogy of 'hook, line and the sinker'. You can help them to identify:

- the *initial hook* – in this case, the belief that they have been insulted. The hook is: 'This guy has just insulted me. He has disrespected me.'

- the *line* – the train of thoughts that might occur in such a situation. These might be:

    1. 'He has insulted my mother. He has insulted my whole family.'

    2. 'I don't believe he said that. He will never say that again.'

    3. 'Who does he think I am? I will show him who I am.'

    4. 'Your mother too!'

- the *sinker* – the feelings or emotions experienced, which allowed the hook to sink in and take hold much deeper. The sinkers underpinning each thought might be, for example:

    1. 'He is showing me no respect.'

    2. 'To insult a man's mother is the worst thing.'

    3. 'If I back off now he will never respect me, nobody will respect me.'

    4. 'My family would expect me to teach him a lesson.'

If there are a large number of participants, it is a good idea to try this exercise in two smaller groups to give more people a chance to run through it with one of their own 'Red Rag' situations. Each group will need the support of an experienced facilitator to hold the process and any emotional reactions it may arouse.

Feedback

Some questions to ask are: 'What things did you observe in this exercise? What did you notice that was similar to how you behave in such situations in real life? How can this process be useful to you? How can being able to identify the hook, the line and the sinker help us in tough situations?'

Some useful back-up questions to ask are: 'How does the initial hook get a hold on us? How does it influence us? In what way does getting hooked start a particular way of thinking, like a chain of thoughts? What kind of power do these thoughts have over us? If you want to "unpack the punch", how does it help you to understand what is going on in any situation?'

COMMENTS

Many people will argue that they don't think, they just react, that things happen so fast that there is no time for thinking anyway: 'I hit first and think or talk later.' This is because they are no longer aware of their thoughts. At some stage in the past, they would have had a train of thoughts directing them to respond in a particular way, but now their reactions have become 'automatic', as if they have a permanent, in-built command to react in a particular way in certain circumstances, and no longer have the ability to think or consider other options.

This exercise plays a valuable role by recreating that thought process, and creating a mental space that enables people to start recovering these thought processes. Make no attempt to resolve or change any of the situations (this occurs on Day 2). The focus in this exercise is clearly on what happens inside us during the process of getting hooked. The more we understand our internal processes, the more control we can exercise in tough situations. The thoughts, feelings and beliefs we have are not silly or stupid, they are just the thoughts/feelings/beliefs we have. We need to accept what is going on inside us, however ridiculous it might seem to others. Keep the group focused on what happens to us, on the key role our thoughts, emotions and beliefs play in any conflict scenario.

Once you feel you have fully grasped this exercise, you could explore alternative ways of structuring it, such as using tableau or frozen images to depict the power of each thought, feeling or belief. Getting the participant to see all the images that are 'living' inside them, can be very effective.

The fixed row of chairs provides the exercise with an initial structure. Once the participants are familiar with the flow of the exercise, you could have the 'thoughts' walking around and speaking just behind the participant who is in the process of getting hooked.

'Getting Hooked' provides us with a foundation for our work on Day 2 of this workshop in the exercises 'Insults and Accusations' and 'Getting Unhooked'. It also links with 'Red Labels' on Day 1 and 'Life Sentence' on Day 3 of the Advanced Leadership Workshop, and the work on choices and consequences in the 'Fear and Fashion' Workshop.

Closing – a large group reflection and feedback exercise

This gives everyone in the group the chance to comment on whatever they have noticed, learnt, or appreciated, or something they have discovered about themselves during the first day. Once they have done so, ask the group if there is anything else anyone would like to say before completing the day.

Ask them if there is anyone who needs some support or would like to talk to one of the facilitators at the end of the session. Ask if there is anyone who will not be attending Day 2. This could be an opportunity to say goodbye to someone and thank them for their participation. End the day with an affirmation for the group in terms of their participation and contribution to the workshop.

FINAL COMMENTS ON THE DAY

At this stage of the workshop it is sufficient just to ask questions during the feedback, leaving the level of responses to the group. It is important to take the group with you by building gently on their level of participation.

Some questions have an effect on their own, even if nobody answers. They begin a thought process or affirm an experience, even if participants choose not to respond at the time. You can be more rigorous later in the process, when you feel the group is sufficiently engaged with the material, and you can challenge them more to explore their responses in greater depth.

You can expect the mood of the group to be varied at the end of Day 1. This is normal. Many participants might still feel wary, testing out the process and the facilitators. Others might display lots of bravado and enjoy the attention they get. Some might feel frustrated or unsettled, especially after the 'Getting Hooked' exercise. The feelings that participants experience when they really 'get hooked' are often present in the workshop after this exercise.

It is also challenging for them to confront the notion that someone or something 'hooks' us, and that we are not always 'in control'. For many, the notion of being able to control people and situations is critical to their survival. The thought of not being in control is extremely threatening, and their attachment to control is the very thing that makes them prone to getting hooked and, in turn, losing control.

By the end of Day 1 we have started to invite participants to take a step outside of this control zone, their comfort zone, to a place where they can discover some personal power for themselves, which is not dependent on their 'control' of the world.

Remember in your end-of-day debrief to reflect on whether there are any support needs emerging for individual participants.

The best way to exercise control is to surrender control, and just let go.
Joanna Bull, Founder of Gilda's Club Worldwide

As far as your self-control goes, as far goes your freedom.
Maria Ebner von Eschenbach

Day 2
Focus: *From the past*

Cracking the act – breaking out

Agenda

Session 3

- Adjective Names
- Dangerous Journey
- Movie Picture Freeze-Frame
- Focus of the Day
- Who am I?
- Wind in the Willows

Session 4

- Cat and Mouse
- Paper and Floor
- Insults and Accusations
- Getting Unhooked
- Closing

Quotes to Introduce the Day

When two elephants fight,
It is the grass which suffers most.
  from Zimbabwe

The axe forgets, the log does not.
  from Zimbabwe

The unexamined life is not worth living.
  Socrates

Session 3

Adjective Names – a warm-up exercise

Ask participants to think of a quality they will bring into the workshop today, and add it to their own name. It should be something they can be expected to contribute to the group, or a specific way in which they will participate. Examples might be 'Listening Lionel' or 'Trusting Sophie'. Go round the circle and give all the participants a chance to share their adjective name and explain why they have chosen it. Encourage them to use what they declared to the group earlier, during the 'Personal Introductions' exercise on Day 1 (see page 61). Also ask them to say how they are feeling about participating today. Check at the end to see if anyone has a specific request to make before continuing the workshop.

COMMENT

Our intention here is to make an immediate link back to yesterday, as well as to the overall theme of the workshop, and also to ensure that everyone gets a chance to speak during the first exercise of the day. We get to do a check on the participants to see if anything needs to be cleared up before beginning a new day.

Dangerous Journey – a team-building and problem-solving trust exercise

Group participants into a team, or teams, of seven. Each team gets four chairs (i.e. half as many chairs as there are participants in each team, plus one). One member of each team wears a blindfold. Explain to participants: 'You are on a piece of land surrounded by molten lava (or toxic waste). You have to cross to a safe 'piece of land' (i.e. cross the room), using the chairs. You cannot touch the floor at any time on the journey. All the team members must cross together at the same time, as the level of molten lava/toxic waste surrounding your piece of land is rising rapidly. Any member falling off a chair is out. You must try to complete the journey with all members alive.'

Give participants five minutes planning time before they start. Observe how the teams plan and work together during the journey.

Feedback

Lead a discussion to reflect on 'Dangerous Journey.' The focus is on teamwork, trust and leadership. Some questions to use are: 'How did you work as a team? What worked? What could have been improved? What was the experience like for the blindfolded participant? What does this say about trust? Who took the lead in the planning stage and in the journey itself? What different types of leadership were used? Did everyone in the team take some kind of a lead? In what ways did everyone take a lead? What does this exercise/experience say to us about leadership? How did your experience of this exercise compare with the 'Trust Circle Walk'? How did those who had blindfolds find the exercise compared to yesterday?'

Movie Picture Freeze-Frame – a small group exercise introducing the freeze-frame technique

Divide the participants into small teams of four or five and ask them to choose a well-known film or TV programme. Each team must think of three dramatic moments from their chosen movie and create them, using each other. They freeze their bodies as if the moment is caught in a photograph or a poster advertising the movie.

The teams prepare their three frozen pictures and then show them to the larger group. After seeing each team, the group tries to guess the title of the movie shown.

COMMENTS

These last two exercises are intended to warm up, relax and ease the participants back into the room, the group and the workshop process.

Focus of the Day

From the past: Cracking the act – breaking out

The focus of Day 2 is to unlock the present from the past in order to create a future that does not resemble the past. Participants will explore the power their past experience holds over their behaviour in the present. They are encouraged to put the past into the past – to learn from the past, but not to be constrained by it.

Introduce the Focus of the Day, linking it to the next exercise, 'Who am I?' You could use a couple of the quotes on page 73 to encourage a discussion around the Focus of the Day.

See Notes for Facilitators: 'Presenting a workshop' and 'Introducing the focus of each day' on page 55.

Who am I? – a personal sharing exercise using the freeze-frame technique

When introducing 'Who am I?', refer to the preceding exercise. Tell the participants: 'A film company has asked you to make a documentary programme featuring your life. Choose two distinct moments from your past that have had an important influence on who you are today – so important that if these scenes were left out, the movie would not truly reflect your life.'

If the workshop numbers are small, then each participant could show three pictures.

Participants prepare their 'frozen pictures' in the same teams as for the last exercise. Each team member must have a turn, using the other team members to create their two pictures. They do not need to go into any detail – simply create the picture and explain to the group who it is that each person is portraying. Participants keep themselves out of their own pictures, and ask another member to represent them.

Each participant thinks of a one- or two-word title for each picture, to describe how they felt when that incident happened – for example, 'Lost' or 'Scared'.

When the pictures are shown to the entire group, participants explain who is there, their age at the time, where they are, what is happening.

Feedback

Some questions to use are: 'What do the pictures we've seen have in common? Which pictures stood out for you? What was it like for you creating your pictures? What was it like to share those with all of us? What was it like being in others' pictures? What was it like seeing the pictures from other people's lives and experiences? What do you get from sharing your life with others? What do you get when others share their lives with you? Did recreating a moment from the past take any of you back into those experiences? What feelings did you experience? Do any of you feel that the pictures you have shown still influence your life today? In what ways? Do any of you feel stuck in those pictures from the past – as if you always have a hook in you, or are hooked to your past? Were there pictures you chose not to show? What would it take for you to share those pictures? How much influence do those pictures have on your life today?'

COMMENTS

The question 'Who am I?' is often a turning point in the workshop in terms of participation, mood and focus. For some this is the real entry point into the workshop. It give them an opportunity to reflect back and remember the past. The frozen images often recreate the emotions and feelings of the event depicted. Because everyone participates in someone else's pictures, an atmosphere of respect for the life experiences of others is created. Participants can choose moments of joyful celebration or profound loss; the choice is theirs. In the introduction they are only asked to choose influential events in their life, no further direction is given. We usually find, especially when working with young people at risk, that the experiences they choose, more often than not, are expressions of pain, loss, grief, betrayal, violence or abuse. The various pictures normally share lots of common ground.

The pictures are moving. The participants tend to be quiet and reflective. The mood of the feedback is often the most intimate and emotional of the workshop. The pace should be slow, voices can be soft, the sharing can be deep. Encourage as many participants as possible to contribute. You might find that the feedback develops gently into a sharing. It is important that enough time is left for feedback and sharing after seeing the pictures.

When you call a break after this exercise, it is a good idea to acknowledge to everyone that emotions might be raw, that people might be feeling sensitive, and it is a good idea to take care of each other over the break and be aware of how others might be feeling.

Wind in the Willows – a group trust exercise

One participant stands with their feet together in the centre of a tight circle. They hold their body stiff and cross their arms over their chest. They let their body drop backwards and allow the group to support their weight. The group passes the person in the middle around and across the circle, like a strong willow tree being blown backwards and forwards in the wind. It is important that the group supports the participant, allowing them to relax. Each participant should have an opportunity to be the 'willow' in the exercise. Facilitators need to keep the group alert, concentrated and focused all the time. It is better if the participant in the middle closes their eyes and the supporting group remains silent.

Feedback

Use questions similar to those for the 'Trust Circle Walk' (see pages 65–66) and adapt them to this exercise. It would be good to acknowledge any differences and individual specific achievements when comparing participation during the 'Trust Circle Walk' yesterday and 'Wind in the Willows' today.

COMMENTS

Checking that the 'protective wall' of participants is ready to support on each new turn is vital. Supporters should be in a relaxed position, with one leg forward and the knee bent in a slight crouch position. (It is very difficult to take someone's weight if you are standing upright with straight legs.) As in the 'Trust Circle Walk', you need to find creative ways of including all participants, in case some find this exercise tough. The level of intimacy and physical contact is increased in this exercise. It is important to keep the participants focused on the person having their turn. A silly remark or laughter is often enough to unsettle a nervous participant.

This trust exercise follows on well from the atmosphere created in 'Who am I?' It serves to reinforce the group cohesion that is emerging. It offers those who might have struggled yesterday in the trust exercise a chance to have another go, and offers a further challenge to those who found the Trust Walk fairly easy.

Session 4

Cat and Mouse – a warm-up game for 'Getting Unhooked'

Two participants stand in the middle of a circle. One plays the cat, and gets a blindfold. The other plays the mouse. Both get a shaker. The object of the game is for the cat to touch the mouse. Every time the cat rattles its shaker, the mouse must reply by immediately rattling theirs. The cat tries to guess where the mouse is, and touch it.

The rest of the participants form a protective circle to ensure that the blindfolded cat doesn't leave the space, and to keep the mouse within the boundaries of the circle. The circle can be large at first and, if the cat is struggling to catch the mouse, it can slowly be drawn tighter to reduce the mouse's space and increase the challenge. Facilitators should encourage everyone to take a turn at playing at least one of the roles.

Feedback

Lead a brief discussion on 'Cat and Mouse'. Ask participants if the relationship between the cat and the mouse reminds them of any of the work done on Day 1. Refer back to 'Bombs and Shields', 'Red Rags' and 'Getting Hooked'. Relate the constant chase of the cat and the avoidance of the mouse to the hooked relationships explored earlier in the workshop. Discuss how the constant rattling of the shakers, the call and the response, can remind us of the tension and strain in a difficult relationship.

COMMENTS

As in the trust exercises, it is important that the 'protective wall' keeps the two participants in the middle of the circle safe. Again, it is best if the 'wall' stays silent, so that the participants can hear clearly and concentrate on the task at hand.

Paper and Floor – a problem-solving exercise to prepare for 'Getting Unhooked'

Facilitators lay out several sheets of newspaper to form a square on the floor – large enough for all the participants to be able to stand on the paper comfortably. Participants start this exercise by standing away from the newspaper, on the floor.

Tell them: 'You must all, at the same time, be in touch with the paper and not with the floor.' Keep repeating this exercise with the same instruction, but each time the group completes it, remove a section of the paper. Continue until the group has only a tiny piece of paper left.

Groups might start using furniture during the exercise. Allow this, but once they have explored this solution, withdraw the use of all objects. Encourage them to find a solution, without helping them to resolve the problem. Encourage them to listen carefully and think creatively at all times.

(*Note*: The exercise is resolved when all participants jump simultaneously off the ground, while holding a piece of the paper.)

Feedback

Lead a discussion to reflect on 'Paper and Floor'. The focus is on how we interpret what is said to us, and the meaning we attribute to things – in this case, the instructions for the exercise.

Some questions to use are: 'What does this exercise say about how we approach problems or challenges? Why did we have to go through the process we did in order to get to the final solution? What does it say about how we hear things? How was the teamwork? What worked? What could be improved? What did you discover about the way you work in a team and the role you play? When do you take a lead, and when do you let others take the lead? When do you withdraw? When do you feel like giving up? When do you actually do give up? When do you get angry, upset or annoyed?'

COMMENTS

Tension levels can rise in this exercise. That is okay. Individuals might struggle in this one and feel a little stupid at being unable to find a solution. They may start to become frustrated. Observe the interactions and mood swings, and use these observations as examples in the work of the rest of the session.

Encourage the participants to 'stay with it' and to have patience. The solution will come, as long as they give it the time and space. It will definitely emerge. Sometimes we find that the solution has already been hinted at by one member of the group, but the suggestion was not heard, taken up or seriously considered by others. The facilitator can gently lead the group forward without providing any solutions.

Insults and Accusations – a role-play demonstration to introduce 'Getting Unhooked'

Ask two participants to play two young people in a brief role-play. Ask one young person to deliver the worst possible insult to the other. Ask the one who has received the insult to say what they would do in the same circumstances – for example: 'I would kill them' or 'I would teach them a lesson'.

Tell the other participants: 'You are witnesses to an assault. Describe what you saw.' Allow all the participants to say what they observed. Their reports will be full of their opinions and interpretations.

Once they have all reported back, ask them what they have given. Have they given the facts of what happened? Ask someone to attempt to give the pure facts of what happened. Work with the group until they have given facts with no judgements attached.

Note: The facts in this case would be, 'One young person said to another young person, "You are…".'

Feedback

Some questions to ask are: 'What have you observed from doing this exercise? How is it that we create the hooks that get us? What is the difference between the judgements, opinions and interpretations we gave, and the pure facts of what happened? In what way can not seeing the facts just as they are, be a dangerous thing? How does it affect us when we make decisions based on our judgements and not on the facts of what is happening?'

COMMENTS

Encourage participants to realise that it is not the person delivering the insult that creates the hook. For example, it is not the person who utters the words, 'You are…!' who creates the insult. An insult is only an insult if we perceive it as one. An accusation is only an accusation if we give it that meaning.

Use the role-play example above to look at the possible consequences for the young person who saw the comment as an insult. Discuss how we do have power over how we respond in any situation, but how we often give that power away. We let our own interpretation of the situation push us into reacting automatically to what we hear. Giving our power away is what leads to us into getting hooked, so actually we hook ourselves. We only find the power to get ourselves unhooked when we take full responsibility for our reactions.

The atmosphere in this session often takes on an entirely different mood from where we left off in Session 3. This now feels like hard work, which it is. It is now a struggle. The participants are beginning to examine and question a whole pattern of behaviour and a way of being. Many of them will not immediately grasp the distinction we are making between facts and interpretations.

It is a tough phase of the workshop. Facilitators must keep faith in the process and persevere. Some participants may be shutting off a little in fear, after the sharing of the last session. The mood can be one of uncertainty, of not understanding where this process is heading. The work done here provides the participants with a critical tool to use, but the understanding does not come easily. Some will struggle with the notion that we hook ourselves: they will still be 'hooked into' the insult, and attached to the meaning that they attach to it. You need to keep them struggling and engaging in the process.

Getting Unhooked – a personal interpretation exercise using freeze-frame technique

Use a situation from one of the pictures shown in 'Who am I?' in Session 3 (pages 75–76) as an example, and from it create four new frozen pictures.

- The first one represents the facts of the situation – for example, 'My father left our family when I was five years old.'

- The second one represents the meaning or interpretation that the participant gave to the situation – for example, 'He didn't love me. My own father didn't think I was worth his love and attention. If my own father doesn't love me, nobody else will. If I can't trust my own father, I can't trust anybody.'

- The third one represents the decision the participant made, based on the meaning they gave – for example, 'Nobody is going to hurt me again. I won't let anybody get close to me ever again.'

- The fourth picture represents the consequences of the decision they took – for example, 'I am lonely. I don't create lasting relationships with anyone. I find it difficult to trust anybody.'

Divide participants into small groups. Each participant selects one of their pictures from 'Who am I?' showing a situation from the past that has had a strong influence on them and which remains unresolved. They use members of their group to create a series of four frozen pictures, as outlined above.

If there is time, ask some of the participants to share their pictures with the larger group. This will provide you with various examples of facts and interpretations and of the different meanings that have been created, as well as examples of the decisions people made and the consequences of those decisions. These examples can be referred to during the reflection.

Feedback

Some questions to use in reflecting on 'Getting Unhooked' are: 'What are some of the ways of behaving you have had to take on in order to survive? What decisions are these based on? What are some of the costs of your decisions? What did you find out by separating the facts from your meanings/interpretations? How can this separation be useful to you? What now becomes available to you, now that you can see the cost of your decisions? What is possible for you, now that you see you created all that meaning, and that your decisions were not based on the facts? What is possible, now that you can see that you created who you are today?'

COMMENTS

In the example above, the decision to act is clearly based on the interpretation the participant made at the time. The interpretation becomes like a 'fact' for the person. This process of 'getting unhooked' enables us to go back, clarify the facts by separating them clearly from our interpretation, and create a different meaning based on the facts.

In this example, it might be a fact that the participant's father did not love them. But the conclusion they drew from this situation, 'If my own father doesn't love me, nobody else will. If I can't trust my own father, I can't trust anybody' is something they made up for themselves, to enable them to make some sense out of the situation and to survive. Now they have the power to return to the facts and reinterpret them. We can never change what has happened, but we can alter what we made it mean, and we can then alter what we have become as a result of our own decisions. We can then release ourselves from the past – and in this way unlock the present in order to create a future.

The key task in this exercise is to separate the pure facts from the meaning that was created out of them. It also helps to identify the decisions that were taken and the consequences of those decisions. It is in this process that participants begin to uncover an act they have been putting on in order to survive, to cover up a past hurt, or something that has been missing from their lives. This process can empower participants, by enabling them to begin to see how they put this act together. Now they are in a position to dismantle it if they choose to – if they want to break out of a particular mould that is restricting them and limiting their opportunities in life.

The themes of 'Cracking the Act' and 'Breaking Out', as well as the work of 'Getting Hooked' and 'Getting Unhooked', are developed and deepened in the Advanced Leadership Workshop.

Closing – a large group reflection and feedback exercise

Provide an opportunity for everyone to say something they learnt or observed about themselves during the day's session. Follow the same procedures as suggested for the closing at the end of Day 1.

FINAL COMMENTS ON THE DAY

If the day has been full of mood swings, that is normal. If the participants are exhausted, that is to be expected. Advise them to get a good rest and reassure them that if they are feeling confused, that is not surprising, given the tough day it has been. Encourage them and tell them that on Day 3 the various strands come together to form a picture that will begin to make some sense. They are in the middle of a process, like being in the middle of watching a film with a complex plot: you don't quite know what is going on, so you need to watch the rest of the movie to find out. They need Day 3 to make some sense of Day 2!

If you're sometimes confused, that's good. It means you're shedding outmoded beliefs but you haven't yet reached new conclusions. You're in a state of flux. But you're progressing, you're questioning, you're going where you haven't been before.

Mike Lipkin

Under all that we think, lives all we believe, like the ultimate veil of our spirits.

Antonio Machado

Day 3
Focus: *For the future*

Taking a stand – moving on

Agenda

Session 5

- Old Sock
- Imagining
- Focus of the Day
- Jailbreak
- Vicious Circle

Session 6

- Building a Future Today
- Boxing Ring
- Taking a Lead in My Life
- Achievements
- Acknowledgements
- Evaluation
- The Next Step
- Closing Ceremony

QUOTES TO INTRODUCE THE DAY

I learned that courage was not the absence of fear,
but the triumph over it.

Nelson Mandela, from Long Walk to Freedom

A word is dead when it is said, some say.
I say it just begins to live that day.

Emily Dickinson

A dog has four feet
but does not travel four roads at once.

from Haiti

Session 5

Old Sock – a warm-up game

Divide the participants into two teams. The teams form a line at opposite ends of the room, so that each member of one team stands directly opposite a member of the other. Give each pair of opposing team members a number. A facilitator stands in the middle of the room at an equal distance from both teams, with one arm outstretched, dangling a sock.

The facilitator calls a number, and the two opponents come forward to grab the sock. If they can grab the sock and get it back to their team without being touched by their opponents, they get a point for their side.

If the one who grabs the sock gets touched on the way back to their team, the point goes to the opposing side. Later in the game, the facilitator could call out two numbers together, so that four participants go for the sock at the same time. If a participant or facilitator is left out of the teams because of an odd number of participants, or physical injury/disability, they could take on the role of referee and/or scorer.

Feedback

Some questions to use are: 'What tactics were used in the game? Which tactics worked particularly well? What did you learn from observing other peoples tactics? In which ways did you adapt what you learnt? What skills did you use when observing or adapting tactics? Is there anything that you discovered in playing this game that you could use in your life as a skill? Did you observe anybody doing the same thing, using the same tactics/methods again and again? Were they achieving a good result for themselves? How difficult is it to change a behaviour, to try something different, when you are already getting great results? What would you say about somebody who was using the same behaviour repeatedly, but not getting the desired result?

COMMENTS

Every warm-up game provides an opportunity to further the themes and focus of the Leadership Workshop. We suggest links and give examples. You may find links and examples that you would like to explore with the participants through your own specific line of questioning. The questions we use are there for the purpose of opening up and exploring a chosen theme or focus. Questioning is most effective when it follows a coherent path.

Imagining – a warm up exercise

Ask participants to imagine what they would choose to be if they were, for example, an animal, a piece of music, a fruit or an implement, and to think why. (The facilitator chooses the theme for the exercise.) Each participant in turn then gives their response – for example: 'If I was an animal I would be an elephant, because I would like to live long and I'd like to have a good memory.'

Other possible themes:

- If I were a parent, the kind of mother/father I would like to be is…
- If I were a leader, the kind of leader I would like to be is…
- If I was an inventor, the kind of inventor I would like to be is…

Feedback

Are dreams necessary? Why do we need dreams? What becomes possible when we imagine who we are, or who we would like to become? What is imagination? What does it mean 'to imagine'? What is so powerful about the imagination? What does it make available to us? What happens when we share our thoughts and dreams with others? What do we create when we have a dream? What do we need in order to continue having a dream? How do we make dreams come true? What prevents us from realising our dreams?

COMMENTS

Our purpose today is to encourage the participants to dream and to imagine what is possible in their lives, and then to build a real foundation to support the dream, so that the hope or the dream can become a reality, and the reality can be sustained.

Focus of the Day

For the future: Taking a stand – moving on

The focus of Day 3 is reaching a vision we have of ourselves in the future by creating it through appropriate action in the present. Participants get an opportunity to practise strategies that will enable them to break out of an existing cycle of behaviour. They will declare what it is they want for their lives, what obstacles might stand in their way, and which first steps they need to take in order to create the future. They experience giving and receiving support.

Use the 'Imagining' exercise on page 85 to lead into a discussion of the day's focus.

You could use a couple of the quotes on page 84 to encourage a discussion around the Focus of the Day.

See Notes for Facilitators: 'Presenting a workshop' and 'Introducing the focus of each day' on page 55.

Jailbreak – a game to prepare for 'Vicious Circle'

For this game you will need an odd number of participants. Divide the group into prisoners and warders so that there is one more warder than there are prisoners. You will need as many chairs as there are warders. Form a circle of chairs and ask each warder to stand behind a chair. Prisoners then sit on the chairs. There will be one warder left without a prisoner.

The object of the game is for the warder with the empty chair to 'steal' a prisoner from one of the other warders. This warder winks at one of the prisoners who then tries to escape from their chair and reach the empty chair without being touched by their current warder. Warders can stop their prisoner escaping by touching them if they think they are about to move. The warders are not allowed to move their feet from a set position at least one foot (30 cm) behind their chairs. They have to stand with their arms behind their backs.

When a prisoner escapes, a new warder will be left with the empty chair, and has to try to fill it by winking at a prisoner. After a while you can swap round so that warders can have a chance to play prisoners and vice versa.

Feedback

Some questions to ask are: 'What was the purpose for the prisoners in "Jailbreak"? What was the purpose for the warders? Did the prisoners really escape? Where did they escape to? Did the warders really have to be concerned about an escape? What would you say about someone who kept on trying to escape but never did? What would you call the thing inside which the prisoner is trapped? Who or what keeps this self-imposed prison, what we call a vicious circle, intact?'

Note: In the course of these questions and discussion, participants normally produce the term 'vicious circle', or similar, which can then be used to describe the next exercise (below). The facilitator can use the discussion to lead into the exercise.

Vicious Circle – based on the participants' contributions and using freeze-frame

Join about four large sheets of paper together, and draw a series of six circles, two larger circles (1 and 4) and four smaller ones (2 and 3, 5 and 6), as shown in the diagram below. (Do not write the numbers inside the circles – they are for ease of reference only.)

Following the sequence below, ask participants to call out their responses to a series of questions. Write up words or phrases from these responses, inside each circle.

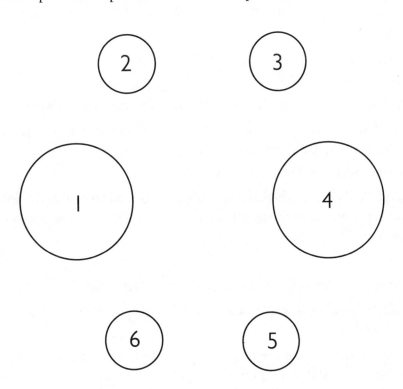

- **Circle 1**
  - Write below the first circle: 'WHAT HAPPENED TO ME'.
  - Ask the participants: 'What happened to you/what happens to people in order to get you/them into a vicious circle in the first place? Who or what was responsible for getting you/others into trouble? Who or what was to blame?'
  - Listen to their responses – for example, 'beaten by my father', 'kicked out by my mother', 'expelled from school', 'had no food', 'pressure from friends' – and write them up in abbreviated form inside the first circle – for example, 'violence', 'expulsion', 'starving', 'peer pressure'.
  - Write above the first circle: 'I GOT DONE TO'.
  - Explain: 'When all these things happen to us, we experience them as though they have been "done to" us, as if we have been the victims of our circumstances.'

- **Circle 2**
  - Write below the second circle: 'WHAT I FELT'.
  - Ask: 'What feelings do you have when you get done to? How do you feel when all this has happened to you?'
  - Call out the specific words written in the first circle, and get responses to some of these – for example, 'angry', 'sad', 'depressed'. Write them down inside the second circle.

- **Circle 3**
  - Write below the third circle: 'WHAT I THOUGHT'.
  - Ask: 'What do you think when one of these things has happened to you? What thoughts do you have when, for example, your father beats you?'
  - Write responses in the third circle – for example, 'I'm worthless', 'I hate you'.

- **Circle 4**
  - Write below the fourth circle: 'WHAT I DID'.
  - Ask: 'What do you do when these things happen to you and you experience these feelings? What action do you take when you have these thoughts?'
  - Write responses in the fourth circle – for example, 'take drugs', 'become violent', 'try to kill myself', 'self-harm', 'steal'.
  - Write above the fourth circle: 'I GOT EVEN'.
  - Explain: 'When all these things happen to us and we feel and think the way we do, we experience a desire to get even, to do something in order to get revenge, to get our own back.'

- **Circle 5**
  - Write below the fifth circle: 'WHAT IT GAINED ME'.
  - Ask: 'What do you get for yourself/what do you gain when you take one of these actions?'
  - Call out specific words written in the fourth circle and get responses – for example, 'escape', 'satisfaction', 'power', 'respect' – and write them down inside the fifth circle.

- **Circle 6**
  - Write below the sixth circle: 'WHAT IT COST ME'.
  - Ask: 'What do you lose/what does it cost you when you take one of these actions?'
  - Again, call out specific words from the fourth circle and get responses – for example, 'freedom', 'health', 'family', 'love' – and write them down inside the sixth circle.

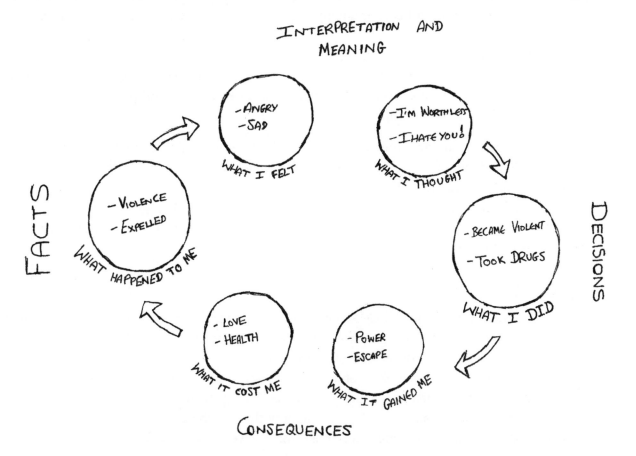

Facilitators should now take the participants through the complete vicious circle. Ask: 'Do you see how the vicious circle works? Do you see how it all fits together? Do you see how it is created? Do you see who creates it?' You don't have to write their responses down – this is merely to check their understanding and to get them to put the vicious circle into their own words.

Facilitators can now relate this exercise to work done on Day 2 in the exercise 'Getting Unhooked' (see pages 81–82). The words written in the first circle (what happened) are the facts. Write 'facts' in big letters down the left side of the Circle 1.

The words written in Circles 2 and 3 (thoughts and feelings) are our interpretation of the facts, the meaning we give to what happened – for example, 'What happened to me is that I got done to.' Write 'interpretation/meaning' in big letters above Circles 2 and 3.

The words written in Circle 5 (the action taken) are the decisions we take – for example, 'I decided to do what I did in order to get even.' Write 'decisions' in big letters down the right side of Circle 4.

The words written in Circles 5 and 6 (costs and gains) are the consequences we live with as a result of our actions. Write 'consequences' in big letters underneath Circles 5 and 6.

Now divide the participants into small groups. In the groups, each participant must first identify a vicious circle they are involved in now, or one they have experienced in the past. If anyone is stuck, encourage them to build on the experiences they used in 'Who am I?' on Day 2.

After they have each shared their vicious circle within their small group (they need only give a brief description, using the structure above – a few words under each heading), ask one participant to volunteer to try to find a way out, or identify an exit point from their vicious circle.

The group then creates a freeze-frame picture for each of the six stages of this participant's vicious circle.

Note: As an alternative to freeze-frame, place six large, clean sheets of paper on the floor with a large, empty circle drawn on each sheet. On each circle write the same titles as in the example described above. Participants can take a turn to stand in each circle and give their own verbal response in each of the six positions (circles).

Group members then discuss: how could the person break out of their circle? At which stage could they have done something which would have enabled them to get out of the circle? What would they have needed to do?

Each small group presents one example of a vicious circle, with suggestions as to the exit point – the way out. The other participants should also be encouraged to contribute their ideas on possible exit points.

Feedback

Lead a discussion on 'Vicious Circle'. The focus is on what the participants have learnt from taking part in the exercise, sharing their experiences with each other, and what they have gained from support from others. Possible questions are:

'What have you learnt from looking at how the vicious circle works? What have you discovered from seeing the vicious circles of others? What can you gain from being aware of your own vicious circles? What becomes available to you, now that you have identified a vicious circle of your own? What support have you given others, or received from others?'

COMMENTS

It is worth taking time over this exercise. This is an opportunity for the participants to draw the different strands of the workshop together, and to begin to make some sense of it for themselves. 'Vicious Circle' provides a powerful tool for understanding what has happened, how it creates a ripple effect that leads us into specific actions, and how these in turn create consequences in our lives. It gives coherence to participants' experiences and actions. They can lay the whole pattern out in front of them, study it, and consider some alternative strategies for themselves.

Session 6

Building a Future Today – an exercise to prepare for 'Boxing Ring'

Ask participants to imagine themselves in ten years' time. What would they like to look back on? What would they like to have achieved in their lives in ten years' time? Each participant gets a chance to respond to these questions. If the responses are brief, ask support questions to get more information.

Now ask participants to think of what their first step would be to achieve their goal: 'What is one thing you could do now that would support you in reaching your goal?' Also ask them to think of the first obstacle that they would need to overcome: 'What is one thing that could stand in your way – like an obstacle – which could stop you achieving your goal?' The questions and answers can be shared in pairs, or in small groups, if time permits.

Ask for volunteers to share examples of their first step and first obstacle in the large group. Then ask for a volunteer who wants to work on taking their first step and overcoming their first obstacle.

Boxing Ring – a structured role-play exercise involving skill development and coaching support

For the 'boxing ring', you need a volunteer with a clearly defined challenge – for example:

- In ten years' time: 'I want to run my own business, a garage.'
- First step: 'I need to complete my school education.'
- First obstacle: 'I must stop stealing and say no to my friends when they ask me to join them.'

Boxing Ring involves a challenger versus an opponent. Ask for a volunteer to play the role of 'opponent' – a friend who tempts our 'challenger' to join them in burgling a house to get some easy money. It is important that the opponent knows and understands the situation involved. Their job is to provide a strong temptation, such that the challenger will be stretched emotionally and psychologically in resisting it.

Ask for two volunteers to act as coaches in the challenger's corner. Their task is to support the challenger during the breaks between rounds, providing positive feedback on how the challenger is doing – what is and what is not working – as well as ideas and strategies to help them resist temptation.

Ask for two more volunteers to act as coaches in the opponent's corner. Their task is to give feedback – for example, whether the challenge is realistic, too easy or too difficult – as well as ideas and strategies for tempting the challenger.

All of the coaches can participate only during the breaks. They may not call out during the rounds.

Other participants can be observers in either of the two corners. Once the role-play is complete, their task is to give the coaches feedback on how appropriate the coaching was – did they give their person too much or too little support? Were they precise and clear? Observers may not participate during the rounds or breaks, and must wait until the end of the exercise to give their comments.

The facilitator plays the role of referee, marking out with chairs an area in which the contest will take place. The referee's task is to call the beginning and end of each round, and to decide how long each round should be. The referee should always know what the challenger is working on in a particular round. If the challenger is having too hard a time, the referee should end the round so that the challenger can return to their corner to receive support from the coaches. If the challenger is clearly succeeding in resisting the challenge, the referee should call the round to an end so that the opponent can get support from their coaches. The referee always sets the scene (where and when it is happening) in consultation with the challenger's corner. The referee tells the participants when the last round is being called.

There is a rule of no physical contact in the boxing ring. The referee must remind the contestants of this. The referee can at any time call a 'freeze' in the action, to give an instruction. Similarly, the challenger can call a 'time-out' and the referee will end the round. The coaches can also indicate to the referee if they feel their fighter needs support from their corner.

All participants should remember that their ultimate purpose is to support the challenger to gain the skills and confidence necessary to overcome the obstacle standing in their way.

The referee gives the two contestants in the ring sticky labels with the names of their characters on them. For example, if the challenger 'John' is playing himself, his role-play name could be 'Just John', if his intention in the exercise is to be true to himself and not to be manipulated. If a participant called, for example, Peter, is playing John's opponent, he could be named 'Manipulating Max'. These names, worn throughout the role-play, remind us of the key intention of each role-player. They also provide us with a useful tool when the role-play is complete. The facilitators can ask each role-player a question in role – for example: 'Manipulating Max, what is one thing you would like to say to Just John before you leave?'

The facilitator can ask them both to remove their labels, once the scene is over, and ask each of them a question – for example: 'As John, what would you like to say to "Just John" if he was still with us?' It is important to end the role-play properly and to bring the challengers, opponents and coaches back out of their roles at the end of the exercise. Remember to welcome them back into the whole group, using their real names.

Feedback

Give each side a chance to discuss the exercise separately. This gives an opportunity for the challenger, the opponent and the coaches to give feedback to each other, and also for the observers in the separate corners to comment. The group then comes back together, and each participant mentions a skill or quality they observed that worked in the exercise. (For example: 'He listened and didn't defend himself,' or 'She remained calm.')

Some questions to ask are: 'What is the value of having a chance to practise your responses in a tough situation? What becomes available to you if you prepare yourself before having to face a difficult situation? What becomes available to you if you create a support system for yourself? What support worked in this exercise? What support didn't work? What was it like giving support to others? What was it like receiving support from others? What was it like working within a supportive environment?'

COMMENTS

It is worth allowing plenty of time for this exercise, providing an opportunity for several participants to take their specific challenge into the ring. With good debriefing after each turn, group members will get more and more effective in their different roles, that is, as opponents or as coaches.

It is vital to acknowledge the skills and qualities displayed in each of the participants' role-plays. These should be linked back to the work of Day 1 in the 'Personal Qualities' exercise (see page 63). Participants need to experience what becomes available to them when they use a specific skill or display a certain quality. They need to gain confidence to do things differently, and to witness the different results that can be produced.

It is also useful to highlight the techniques used by each of the opponents to undermine, manipulate and to hook the challenger. Giving these a name makes them easier to recognise and deal with.

Taking a Lead in My Life – a personal reflection and planning exercise to use in completing the workshop

Each participant fills in their own Leadership Plan (see page 94) and writes their responses to the questions.

COMMENTS

Most participants will need some coaching from the facilitators to complete their responses. Some might need support in writing. Some participants might need to continue to work on their responses after the workshop. It is good to see that a specific time and support process is set up for this to happen. Participants value leaving the workshop with something tangible and clear to work on. This exercise develops their planning skills and demands clarity.

✓

Taking a Lead in My Life

Leadership Plan for ....

A goal I would like to achieve is...

The first step I need to take to achieve my goal is...

I will take this first step by...[date]

Something that might stop me achieving my goal is...

The action I will take in order not to be stopped is...

Someone who will support me in achieving my goal is...

I would like them to support me by...

Achievements – a reflection exercise to use in completing the workshop

In pairs, participants share something they achieved for themselves in this workshop. Facilitators remind them of the skills (from Day 1 – see page 63) that they said they wanted to improve over these three days. Ask some of them to share their accomplishments with the whole group.

Acknowledgements – a group personal-feedback exercise to use in completing the workshop

The whole group stands in a tight circle. Select a participant, and ask three members of the group to give them an acknowledgement. The next person in the circle then receives three acknowledgements – and so on. The person receiving the acknowledgement does not reply – they just listen to what is being said. This gives participants an opportunity to thank each other for the way in which they participated, for the support that they gave, for a quality that others appreciated, or for something that others admired about them.

Evaluation – a feedback exercise to use in completing the workshop

This is an opportunity for participants to give the facilitators feedback on the strengths and weaknesses of the Leadership Workshop. This can be done verbally as a wordstorm and written up on a large sheet of paper so that their comments can be recorded.

Create columns: 'Things I liked'; 'Things I didn't like'; 'Ideas for next time'.

This is not a time for discussion, agreements or disagreements. The participants' comments are simply written up. Evaluation sheets could also be handed out for individuals to complete.

The Next Step – giving information and gathering ideas

Facilitators can give information about opportunities available for participants to continue this training and to practise and develop their skills. Participants might have ideas on how this work could be developed. They might also want to make specific requests to the staff, regarding future participation, support, etc.

Closing Ceremony – completing the workshop

It is a good idea to have certificates available to hand out to participants who took part in all sessions of the workshop. A guest could be invited to give a brief talk on leadership and present the graduates with their certificates. It is also a good idea to close the workshop with an inspirational poem or piece of writing. It is best to invite one of the participants to read it out in front of the whole group.

If possible, hold a closing ceremony or a certificate ceremony once every few months, and invite siblings, parents, friends and staff from the partner agencies. This spreads the idea of the programme to a larger audience, and allows the participants to be acknowledged publicly.

FINAL COMMENTS ON THE DAY

Participating in this process in just three days is a very intense experience. The material shared in this workshop could easily expand to fill six days. Then the work could go a lot deeper, and participants would have more time to absorb the material and greater opportunity to share and try out the exercises, making for a richer experience. It would also allow other activities to be scheduled in between, providing relaxation and relief from the intensity this work generates.

If three days is all you have, you can still make the very best use of this opportunity. You just need to accept that you can only do so much in the time available. You get to wherever you get, and the participants gain whatever they gain from the experience. You provide the very best opportunity for them to participate, and the rest is up to them.

It's easier to say what we believe than be what we believe.

Dr Robert Anthony

Chapter 7
The Advanced Leadership Workshop

Introduction to the Advanced Leadership Workshop

The Advanced Leadership Workshop aims to deepen and strengthen the process that has been started in the Leadership Workshop. It focuses on aspects of listening, acknowledgement, supporting, honesty and self-questioning. As with the Leadership Workshop, the Advanced Leadership Workshop works best when the participants have chosen to participate.

When participants volunteer for the Advanced Leadership Workshop, their experience of the other workshops should give them a good idea of what to expect – and it is reasonable to expect from them a high level of participation. The Advanced Leadership Workshop aims to provide participants with more of a challenge, so that they can stretch themselves beyond the 'comfort zones' that they are used to and where they are comfortable. This workshop, like the other workshops, works best when delivered as a block, rather than in weekly sessions. The material as presented here requires at least six hours (two three-hour sessions) each day. These times do not include short breaks and meal breaks. However, in community programmes young people may be unable to commit to a whole day, and so the material can be reorganised to suit different settings, according to the needs of the group.

The Advanced Leadership Workshop should be facilitated by staff who have built up confidence and experience with the other workshops. This will give them a natural feel for what their particular young people need to develop their leadership role within the programme.

The workshop focus

Much of the introduction to the Leadership Workshop also applies to the Advanced Leadership Workshop. Although the journey of exploration that participants will undertake is again focused on the past, the present and the future, the focal points for each day are different, so as to strengthen and deepen the work.

- **Day 1** focuses on the labels participants are given by others in the present, and the labels they give themselves. Participants are introduced to the idea of 'Acts' (see below for a more detailed description). They are asked to identify their usual Acts and explore the costs and gains of a particular Act.

- **Day 2** asks participants to examine the history of their Acts. They explore how an Act is assembled on the basis of past events, and identify core beliefs they hold about themselves and the world, which fuel their Acts, limit their thinking, and limit the choices available to them.

- **Day 3** focuses on how participants can step out of these Acts, so that they are no longer compelled by them and can move on. Participants will learn a practical tool to express the feelings behind an Act, which will enable them to give up the Act and create powerful and direct communications.

Acts

The main focus of this workshop is on 'Acts'. In this context, an Act is both the habitual behaviour that we present to the world and which others see and hear, and the internal patterns of thought that keep that habitual behaviour fixed firmly in place. Other words that might be used to describe an Act are 'mask', 'front', and 'attitude'. You may well be able to think of more. We all have Acts.

When we are locked into these habitual patterns of thought and behaviour, it is often very hard for us to step outside them and reflect on their impact on our lives. Referring to them as 'Acts' is a tool to help us do this. It enables us to identify our behaviour as separate from ourselves, and so to see it more clearly. The Acts that we use every day are often the hardest for us to identify, as we are too close to them. It is easier to give up an Act when we can see clearly that it is costing us something, just as it is easier to stop smoking when we realise that we can't run as fast as we used to.

This workshop is concerned with the Acts that limit young people's choices, so that they always respond to difficult or challenging situations in a way that is destructive or damaging to themselves or others. For many of the young people we work with, their Acts are all they have to protect themselves from their own intense feelings of vulnerability and hurt. This work is an extreme challenge for them, and as a facilitator, you will need to exercise compassion and sensitivity.

Another aspect of Acts is as signs of a time when we got 'stuck' – when something happened, when someone did something either to us or that we witnessed, and we made it mean something. We then became 'stuck' with that meaning, so that it is now the filter through which we see the world or ourselves. Our Acts are just outward manifestations of that inner 'stuckness'.

Working on Acts can be like working on the layers of an onion. You peel one Act away, and you find another underneath, and so on. The reason for working on our Acts is not to rid ourselves of them. That is impossible; they will always be with us, one way or another. The purpose is to free ourselves of the hold our Acts have over us, and so gain power and choice in our lives.

The course can be seen as an *inquiry* into Life and how we choose to lead it, with the following questions used as focus points during the workshop.

- **How do I present myself?** What do I hide? How do I hide it? What do I hide behind? How do others view me? How do I view myself? How much of myself do I allow others to see? What are the parts of me I never allow others to see?

- **What choices do I make?** How do I know when I'm making a choice and not acting out a habit? What are the signs that I am operating out of an Act? When do I not practise choice? What supports me in practising choice?

- **What things do I have the power to change?** What *don't* I have the power to change? What *do* I have the power to change? What do I *choose* not to change? *When* do I choose not to change? What do I believe about my power to change things? Who has the power – me or my Acts?

- **Where do I get stuck/unstuck?** When did I first become stuck? What do I believe about getting stuck? What do I make it mean? How do I get unstuck? What support do I need to get unstuck?

Clearings

Days 2 and 3 of this workshop begin with a 'clearing'. A clearing is a space in the workshop for participants to clear up anything they need to clear up, either with other participants or with a facilitator, so that they can participate fully in the work of the day. It is literally a time for them to 'clear the way' for their own participation. It can also be used by facilitators to raise issues around participation that need to be addressed, such as the consistent breaking of a group guideline. It can also be a time for participants to reflect on and articulate their previous learning, to prepare themselves for the day to come.

Important things to think about when introducing the Advanced Leadership Workshop

It may be some time since participants have attended a workshop, and they may need a reminder of what they will be doing, the role of facilitators, how they can get the most out of the workshop, practical issues, and housekeeping. We recommend that you re-read the introduction to the Leadership Workshop (see pages 57–58), as much of that also applies to the Advanced Leadership Workshop. (You may want to repeat parts of it in your introduction to the Advanced Workshop.)

The facilitation methods, exercises, discussions, and games used are all very similar to those in the Leadership Workshop, but you should not assume that participants will remember the details clearly. You will need to spend time establishing a safe and supportive atmosphere. It is possible that not all members of the group have attended the same workshops previously, so they may have no prior relationship with one another. You will need to pay attention to this and work to develop trust and safety in what may, essentially, be a new group.

All members of the group will have participated in at least one Leadership Workshop, and some may have participated in two. Some may have completed the 'Fear and Fashion' Workshop on knife awareness, or the Leadership in Action workshop to train as a group leader. Some may have grown comfortable, even blasé, about the style and content of the Leadership Programme. It is important that the facilitators begin to set a tone for the Advanced Workshop that encourages participants to move beyond their established 'comfort zones' and to engage deeply with the course. You may want to say the following when you talk about participation:

'As in other workshops, what you put into this workshop is what you will get out. If you put a lot in, you will get a lot out. We want to encourage you to really notice how you participate. Notice the times you get bored, or irritated, or check out of the work. Notice the times you feel tired or hungry, or on the edge of your seat with excitement. One of the challenges of this workshop is to be very open about your level of participation. We invite you to inquire into your participation. What is happening that provokes these different reactions in you?

We also invite you to take more risks in this workshop than you did in other workshops. Try everything. Try being first to volunteer, if you are usually last – or last, if you are usually first. Try speaking a little, if you usually speak a lot – or a lot, if you usually speak a little. See how many habits you can become aware of over the three days, and notice how many times you can break a habit. Everyone will really gain from you sharing this. If you really go for this workshop, you will get an enormous amount from it.'

Day 1

Focus: *In the present*

Who am I? – What are my Acts?

The labels I've been given – The labels I've given myself – The Acts I've become

Agenda

Session 1

- Gathering
- Introduction to the Workshop
- About Me
- Group Guidelines
- Trust Run
- Labels Wordstorm
- Focus of the Day
- Red Labels

Session 2

- Posters
- Mime the Lie
- The Act Game
- My Stock Acts
- Act on the Scales
- Poster Time
- Through the Rushes
- Closing

QUOTES TO INTRODUCE THE DAY

If I didn't define myself for myself, I would be crunched into other people's fantasies for me and eaten alive.

Audre Lorde

He who knows others is wise; he who knows himself is enlightened.

Lao-Tzu

The life which is not examined is not worth living.

Plato

You get treated in life the way you train other people to treat you.

Dr Robert Anthony

Session 1

Gathering – an exercise to focus and gather the group

This exercise aims to focus all the participants, to reconnect them with the experience they had last time, and to enable them to share some of the expectations or reservations they might now have. Each participant gets a chance to introduce themselves and respond to the following questions:

- How did you feel when leaving the last workshop?
- How do you feel coming back into this workshop today?
- What do you expect from this Advanced Leadership Workshop?

Introduction to the Workshop

This introduction should cover the same points as suggested in the Leadership Workshop (see pages 57–58). However the focus and intention of the Advanced Leadership Workshop is obviously different (see the introduction to this chapter). When introducing the workshop, it is a good idea to remind participants of the intention and aims that were shared in the first workshop. This is best done by asking them to explain what they actually did and achieved in the last workshop.

About Me – a personal sharing exercise

Ask participants to write down ten important statements about themselves. The statements can be about events that have happened in their lives, events they feel have influenced them in the past, and influence them now; things they hope, feel, think or believe about themselves; things they feel they are or are not; things they find difficult to share with others, but which are nevertheless true. For example, a list might contain statements such as:

- I am 21 years old.
- I have been in prison.
- I am strong minded.
- My father beat me when I was a child.
- I have a two-year-old daughter.
- I think I am quite a weak person.

In pairs, ask participants to share whatever they want to share from their list with their partner. Ask participants to share up to three of the things on their list with the whole group.

Feedback

Some questions to ask are: 'What was it like sharing your information? What was it like listening to someone else's personal information? How much were you willing to share? How much did you risk? What did you risk? Did anyone tell their partner something they didn't tell the large group? Are there things on your list you are not prepared to share with your partner, or with the group?'

COMMENTS

The way you introduce this exercise will determine the nature of the information participants write about themselves. Encourage them to write things they feel, think, or care deeply about, so that their list contains statements that matter to them, rather than a list of things they could easily share with anybody. Reassure participants that they will have complete control over what they share or don't share. Some of the information participants share about themselves will feed directly into the work later on in the day, when they will identify labels and 'Acts' for themselves. This exercise also provides the groundwork for the next exercise – 'Group Guidelines'.

Group Guidelines – an exercise to formulate group guidelines

Ask participants to reflect on their own about what kind of behaviour and attitudes they need from other group members in order to feel comfortable with sharing most or all of the information on their lists. How do they need others to act towards them? What behaviour would encourage them to share themselves? What behaviour would silence them?

In the same pairs as before, ask participants to identify some of the behaviour and attitudes they need to feel comfortable about sharing information in the group.

Ask each pair in turn to feed back to the whole group one guideline they would like the group to adopt. Check with the whole group if the suggested guideline is clear and if everybody agrees to it. Write each guideline up once it is agreed.

COMMENTS

This exercise is part of the process of building a safe and supportive atmosphere in the workshop. It is important that a thorough and rigorous discussion takes place to explore the specific behaviour which encourages full and open participation, and the specific behaviour that hinders it. This begins to set the tone for an Advanced Workshop, as it encourages participants to take full responsibility for their behaviour and the way it affects the atmosphere and others in the room.

Trust Run – a group trust exercise

A trust exercise is recommended for each day of the Advanced Workshop. The trust exercises in this workshop build on the trust exercises in the Leadership Workshop, but provide more of a challenge.

Participants form a protective line against the wall at one end of the room. One participant nominates two others to be the catchers, and a third to be the safety person. The catchers stand just in front of the line, and the safety person stands just in front of them and to the side. The first participant stands at the opposite end of the room, and runs, with eyes closed, towards the wall. As they draw near the wall the safety person shouts 'Stop!', and the catchers prevent them from running into the wall.

Encourage all participants to have a go. We recommend that the facilitator should have experienced this exercise as a participant, and be experienced in leading trust exercises in general. Safety and clear instructions are vital.

Feedback

Some questions to ask are: 'What was that like? How hard/easy is it to trust others with your physical safety? Is it easier/harder to share your feelings and thoughts with others than your physical safety? Did anyone take a real risk in trust? How much did you trust the catchers and the safety person? Did you really allow them to support you, or were you anticipating the wall for yourself? How comfortable/uncomfortable is it for you to trust others with your well-being? Did anyone really put themselves in the hands of their supporters? Is being supported always comfortable? What kind of support in life can sometimes be uncomfortable? What do you usually do when you feel uncomfortable? What feelings do you not like to feel?'

COMMENTS

Encourage participants to start to make connections between how much they will trust others physically and how much they trust others emotionally. With trust exercises such as these it is often surprising how participants who appear physically 'tough' and confident on the surface find it hard to trust others with their physical safety. In this exercise they may be the ones who stop yards short of the safety wall, or find it impossible to run with their eyes shut. If you have time, you can allow participants to have more than one go, to see if they can challenge themselves a little more each time they do the run. It's also important that you do not allow the exercise to develop into a demonstration of bravado. Each participant needs to be affirmed and encouraged to set their own challenge for themselves. For example, for one participant it may be a challenge to just walk down the room with their eyes closed; for another, it will be allowing the safety person to tell them when to stop, rather than stopping themselves short of the safety wall.

Labels Wordstorm – a large group exercise

You will need two large sheets of paper. On one of the sheets write 'What others say.' On the other sheet write 'What I say'. Participants then call out their responses to the following questions:

- What do others say about you and who you are?
- What are the labels that others give you?

Write their responses on the sheet marked 'What others say'. Participants then call out their responses to the following questions:

- What are the labels you give yourself?
- What do you say about yourself and who you are?

Write their responses on the sheet marked 'What I say'.

COMMENTS

When participants refer to their 'reputation', 'identity', 'personality', 'character', it is likely that they are referring to something that is strengthened, defined or created by a label. Labels can be both the names we call ourselves, and the names that others call us. These others could include the police, the media, prison officers, teachers, social workers, family, friends and peers. The list might include terms such as 'criminal', 'stupid', 'slut', 'evil', 'excluded', 'a waster', 'clever', 'wifey', 'teenage mum', 'gangster', 'brethren', 'loyal', 'good friend', etc.

This exercise is a chance to introduce the Focus of the Day, creating a distinction between what others say or believe about us, and what we say or believe about ourselves. Encourage participants to get as much as possible onto the paper, as you may find this wordstorm useful for reference at different points in the workshop.

Focus of the Day

In the present: Who am I? – What are my Acts?

Participants will examine their responses to what others say about them, and explore their reactions to particularly hot or 'red' labels in depth. They will also examine the things that they say or believe strongly about themselves. They will identify the acts they use habitually and that often cost them their feelings, relationships, jobs, and sometimes their freedom. (See pages 98–99 for a detailed discussion of Acts.) The work on Acts will begin in the afternoon session, and will form the basis of the remainder of the workshop.

Discuss the Focus of the Day, linking it to the previous exercise. You could use some of the quotes on page 101 to introduce the Focus of the Day.

Red Labels – a large group sharing and role-play exercise

In the middle of the room lay out pictures and headlines from magazines, books or newspapers. These should relate in some way to labels that members of the group have been given by others. There should be plenty of them, so that every participant has a range of choices.

Each participant chooses an image, and shares with the large group what the image means to them in terms of a label they have been given. What they say may relate to who labelled them, or how they felt when they were labelled.

Then ask participants to choose a label that others have given them that makes them 'see red', that is, a label which they dislike, get irritated by, or get hooked into. Ask them to prepare a short role-play with a partner that shows them receiving the label, and their reaction to it.

Each participant shares their role-play with the rest of the group. After each scene ask the participant who created it to give a one-word title that best describes how they feel about that scene.

Feedback

Some questions to ask are: 'What is it like to be labelled? Is there any truth in the labels others give us? What is the effect of being given the same label throughout your life? Do you live up to your label? Have any of the labels given to you by others stuck with you? Can you choose not to live up to a label? Do you ever feel you have become your label? Why do others label us? Why do we label ourselves? What are the consequences of labels when we label someone else? What are the consequences when someone labels us, or when we label ourselves? Do any of the labels you give yourself empower you? Do any of the labels others give you empower you? Which of your labels limit you?'

COMMENTS

Participants will have a range of different reactions to individual labels. There may be labels they dislike, feel ashamed of, feel proud of, or aspire to. This exercise can bring up strong feelings of anger and injustice for participants who feel that they have been labelled unfairly. It is important to affirm and acknowledge these feelings, whilst encouraging participants to explore their own responsibility in taking on the labels that others give them. Labels that may, at first, seem to empower you can also be the labels that limit you, and vice versa. Acknowledging an element of truth in a label you resist can be the first move in stepping out of someone else's definition of you.

Session 2

Posters – a personal reflection exercise

Hang large blank sheets of paper on the walls – one for each participant. Put a participant's name at the top of each sheet.

Explain to participants that by the end of the workshop the poster will represent their journey through the workshop. It will be something physical that they can take away with them to remind them of the experience. It is up to them what they write on the paper, and they can write as little or as much as they like. The rule is, *they can only write on their own piece of paper*, no one else's. Tell them they will be given opportunities to add to their posters during the three days.

Give them an opportunity now to write something about the morning. This could be a record of some of their 'red' labels. They could attach the images from the morning's exercise to the paper.

COMMENTS

Encourage participants to make these posters their own. They can use words, pictures, graphics and diagrams to convey the sense of their journey. The posters can also be a useful tool for the facilitator, for reminding a participant of what they have already said or discovered about themselves, and providing a clue to a powerful Act that the participant uses in their life.

Mime the Lie – a warm-up game

Participants stand in a circle. A volunteer steps into the middle of the circle and carries out a short mime, such as cleaning their teeth. The next participant steps into the centre and asks what they are doing. The first participant then lies about what they were doing, saying, for example, that they were abseiling down a mountain! The participant who asked the question then has to mime the lie, pretending to abseil down a mountain, and the participant next to them then steps into the circle and asks what they are doing. Continue round the circle until everyone has lied and mimed.

Feedback

Some questions to ask are: 'How often do we *do* one thing and *say* another? How often do we *say* one thing and *do* another? When have your actions not matched your words? How often do we pretend we feel one thing when actually we feel something else – for example, pretend we're fine when really we're hurt, or act aggressively because we are frightened inside? What happens if this becomes a habit? If we are hiding our feelings, what do we show to people?'

COMMENTS

If we habitually hide one side of ourselves whilst showing another, what others see is our Act. This exercise is a useful introduction to the idea of Acts – what we habitually show the world, and what we habitually hide.

The Act Game – a game to introduce the idea of Acts

Ask participants to think of the 'Acts' they see others put on, or that they put on themselves. Ways to describe an Act are: a front or an attitude that you adopt because you don't want others to know what you are really thinking or feeling; or a mask that you wear. (See pages 98–99.)

Write up the all the Acts that participants suggest.

Ask participants to think of something each Act might habitually entail, and a gesture or physical stance the Act might habitually adopt. Write up some words and a gesture for each Act. Here are some examples.

Act	What the Act says	What the Act does
Mr Cool	'It doesn't bother me.'	Shrugs shoulders, looks uninterested.
Poor Me	'I always get blamed.'	Eyes downcast, rounded shoulders, looks small.
Ms Tough	'What's your problem?'	Points, looks aggressive, eyes staring, looks threatening.

Explain that you are now going to play a game with the Acts. Choose five of the Acts that are, for the purposes of the game, significantly different from each other in their physical representations.

Ask one volunteer to form a frozen physical image of one of the Acts, based on what has already been decided about the Act. The image can be a caricature to demonstrate its essence. Ask for two more volunteers to stand on each side of the first one, to form images of the Act's sidekick. The two sidekick images are the same, as mirror images of each other. These images complement the central image, so that you end up with a triptych of images.

Form a circle with the participants. Somebody starts off in the centre of the circle. They point to any member of the circle, and name one of the five chosen Acts. The person indicated must immediately spring into the central image of the act, and the participants on either side of them represent the sidekicks. If any of the three makes a mistake, hesitates or moves too slowly, they end up in the middle. Continue the game until it is impossible to catch anybody out.

Feedback

Some questions to ask are: 'What was that exercise like? What is it like to see the Acts exaggerated? Did you observe anything about yourself during the game? Do Acts have sidekicks in real life? How much does the Act need the sidekicks? How much do the sidekicks need the Act? What is the difference between being a friend to someone and being a sidekick? In your life, how many of your friends are really your sidekicks? Did you spot the Acts of your friends in this exercise? Do your friends and you have any Acts in common?'

COMMENTS

Participants can have a lot of fun with this game. Through the gentle parody of their own habitual behaviours, and those of others, they can begin to separate themselves from their Acts.

Many Acts rely on an appreciative audience of sidekicks. When the sidekicks are removed, it can become easier for someone to drop the Act. If you have time, it may be interesting to reflect on the role of the sidekick as distinct from the role of a friend. The role of a sidekick is to keep someone in their Act, whereas a friend might challenge or support someone to drop the Act.

Often people who share the same Acts join together, forming an 'Act Club'. They will keep each other in their Acts and reassure each other that their ways of behaving, thinking and feeling are the only possible reactions to the different situations in which they find themselves.

My Stock Acts – a personal sharing exercise using the freeze-frame technique

Ask participants to identify three of the Acts they use the most, from the earlier Acts wordstorm.

Divide participants into pairs. Participants sculpt their partners into a frozen image of each of their three Acts. Ask participants to give each Act a one- or two-word title.

Each participant then shares their three Acts and titles with the whole group. After each pair has done this, ask them to write their three stock Acts up on their posters.

Feedback

Some questions to ask are: 'What is your favourite Act? Which Act do you like the most, use the most, or are more reluctant to admit? Which of your Acts gets you into the most trouble? Which of your Acts is most successful? How do your Acts operate together?'

COMMENTS

This exercise can be fast-moving. It helps participants to identify their own Acts and to see others in the room identify theirs. It is another support tool that facilitators can use at other points in the workshop if they see a participant going into one of their Acts.

We usually have two or three favourite Acts that can operate together. As one Act is discarded or confronted, another one comes in to take its place. So, for example, someone may be presenting their 'Ms Tough' Act. If this isn't getting them what they want, they may flip into their 'Poor Me' Act. If this isn't successful, they may slip into their 'Ms Flirt' Act. So a cycle of Acts can develop. If you have time you can explore this with participants to identify situations where they slip habitually from one Act into another.

Act on the Scales – a personal sharing exercise using freeze-frame technique

Ask participants to choose one of their Acts to work on: the Act that costs them the most, for example, or the Act that would be hardest to give up because of what it gains them.

Ask participants to divide into threes and to sculpt pictures of the *costs* and *gains* of their Acts. Each participant represents their own Act, and sculpts one of the other participants into a picture of the gains and the other into a picture of the costs. For example, if a participant is working with their 'Mr Joker' Act, they may gain popularity. What the Act costs them might include their feelings, or real friendship.

Ask participants to think of a one- or two-word title for their gains picture, and another for their costs.

Share the pictures with the whole group. Ask for volunteers to step in and assume the central Act picture each time, so that the participant who is sharing has an opportunity to see their own pictures from outside the tableaux.

Ask the following questions of each participant as they share their pictures: 'What act are we seeing? What are the titles for your pictures? Which is greater, the cost or the gain, and which are you most aware of when you are in your Act? Do you want to change the position of the costs and the gains pictures to show the relationship between them and the Act more clearly?'

For example, a participant working with his 'Mr Joker' Act might begin by placing the costs and gains on either side of the Act, at an equal distance from the main figure. After reflecting on his pictures, the participant might want to move the cost picture (feelings) away from the main picture and the gains picture (popularity) right in front of the Act picture. This would demonstrate that when he is inside his Act, he is completely unaware of what it is costing him because he is so focused on the gains.

Feedback

When everyone has shared their pictures, lead a discussion about the exercise. The following questions could be used: 'What was doing that exercise like for you? When are you more aware of the costs of your Act? When are you more aware of the gains? Are there times in your life when you have tried to give up this Act? What was that like for you? How hard would it be for you to give up what you gain from the Act? Who controls your Act? Do you control your Act, or does your Act control you?'

Note: In the second part of this exercise, where participants work on their costs and gains pictures, the aim is to change the relationship between the three pictures to reflect the participants' view of the relationship accurately, rather than to change the pictures themselves. In the example given above, you would allow the participant to move the costs picture into the corner and the gains picture in front of the Act picture, but you wouldn't allow them to change the cost, gain or Act pictures into different images. Changing or adding to the pictures themselves begins a whole other piece of work that could be developed if you have time.

COMMENTS

If an Act is costing us a lot in our life, and yet we persist in it, it is usually because we have become addicted to the gains. When we become addicted to what An act gets us we become unable to exercise any choice in whether or not we use the Act. This is a point you may want to return to at a later point in the workshop. It may be a question you want to ask in a clearing or something you remind the coaches of in 'Personal Destroyers' on Day 3 (pages 131–133).

This exercise may be very uncomfortable for a lot of the participants. The way they walk, talk, and behave in the world may be one giant Act or cycle of Acts. As far as they are concerned they *are* Mr Gangsta, Ms Tough, Mr Cool, Ms Joker, etc. The idea of giving up an Act will be very tough for them, as it means giving up their entire way of being. Keep affirming them and encouraging them to reflect on the costs and gains of their Act. Remind them they can choose whether or not they work on giving up an Act. Only by getting to grips with the Acts they have assumed and how they control their lives, will they be able to exercise any choice over when, how, and where they use them. Only then will they be able to control their Acts, instead of their Acts controlling them.

Poster Time

Give participants an opportunity to write up any reflections they have on the afternoon's work.

Through the Rushes – a group trust exercise

Participants stand facing each other in two straight lines, with their arms outstretched in front of them and their fingertips almost touching the person opposite them.

A volunteer stands at one end of the line, facing down the line of outstretched arms (the 'rushes'). With eyes closed, the volunteer walks through the rushes. The arms form a gentle barrier which gives way as the volunteer walks through. When the volunteer comes to the end of the line, they are stopped gently. Someone else volunteers, and takes their place in the line. Continue until everyone has had a go.

Feedback

'How did you find that exercise compared to this morning's trust exercise? In what way was it harder? In what way was it easier? Has anything you've experienced today created more trust in you? What was it? How did it create trust in you?'

COMMENTS

As with this morning's trust exercise, encourage everyone to have a go. Some participants might find this gentler, quieter, less dramatic form of trust exercise harder than the apparently more risky 'Trust Run'.

Closing – a large-group reflection and feedback exercise

This is an opportunity for everyone in the group to comment on whatever they have noticed, learnt, appreciated or discovered about themselves during the day.

You could ask participants to comment honestly on their level of participation during the day, or to reflect on the moments they have checked in or checked out, felt uncomfortable, irritated, etc.

Final comments on the day

The Advanced Workshop is a step on from the first workshop and, as such, it should be more consistently challenging. It should be fun, but participants should be worked with more rigorously.

Where participants and facilitators know each other, it is sometimes harder to recreate the mixture of anticipation, apprehension and excitement that both facilitators and participants may have experienced before the Leadership Workshop. To recreate this you may need to challenge some participants hard on this first day to set the tone for the rest of the workshop. You may need to create some low-level discomfort or stretch in participants to cut through any complacency that may be present.

As in the first workshop, it is important to affirm and acknowledge participants' feelings of discomfort whilst encouraging them to stick with these feelings rather than react out of them. In this way they will be able to extend the range of possibilities available to them in terms of their responses to different situations, and create more learning for themselves in the workshop.

It is worth noting that this workshop, as well as being more challenging for participants, is also considerably more challenging for facilitators. You will need to be vigilant in spotting participants' Acts and working with them when they present themselves, as they certainly will, during the workshop. When participants start working on their Acts, those Acts usually begin to pop up in the room! Some participants will struggle enormously, and you will need to go gently with them, affirming and acknowledging their struggle. You will need to encourage all participants to step outside of their 'comfort zone', to take risks, and to inquire deeply into why they are who they are.

By the end of the day there will be a range of feelings in the room, from excitement and interest to apprehension and uncertainty. All being well, everyone will be feeling that they have embarked on a new and intense stage of the Leadership Programme journey of discovery. Tell participants that there will be an opportunity to clear out any leftover feelings from the day in the Clearing the next morning. Thank participants and affirm everyone's participation.

Man can learn nothing except by going from the known to the unknown.
                                                                Claude Bernard

Only those who have already experienced a revolution within themselves can reach out effectively to help others.

                                                                Malcolm X

Day 2
Focus: *In the past*

The history of my Acts – the sentence I created

Agenda
Session 3

- Clearing
- Participation Names
- Fact, Fiction, Faction
- Focus of the Day
- Assembling the Act
- History of the Act
- Poster Time

Session 4

- Count to Twenty
- Nine Dots
- Life Sentence
- Poster Time
- Trust Pictures
- Closing

Quotes to Introduce the Day

Where is the power? Not on the outside, but within… Thoughts are things. You are the thinker that thinks the thought, that makes the thing. If you don't like it then change your thoughts. Make it what you want it to be.

Johnny Coleman

The friend of a fool is a fool.
The friend of a wise person is another wise person.

The Husia

Wounds which cannot be seen are more painful than the ones that you can see which can be cured by a doctor.

Nelson Mandela , revisiting Robben Island, Cape Town, South Africa, 11 February 1994

Session 3

Clearing – an exercise for a reflection on the previous day

Explain to participants that you are going to start today and tomorrow with a 'clearing' to 'clear up' anything from yesterday in order to make way for full participation today. Participants may want to clear up something between themselves and another participant or one of the facilitators, speak about how the previous day's work left them feeling, or declare any insights they had overnight.

COMMENTS

A huge amount of learning can take place in the clearing. If participants want to clear up something between themselves and someone else, you should encourage them to speak for themselves and not others, and to own and take responsibility for their thoughts and feelings. Use the language and tools of the Leadership Workshop to facilitate any discussion that takes place. One of the purposes of the clearing is to get participants 'unhooked' from anything that took place yesterday, so that they can participate fully today.

If a participant has something to clear up with one of the facilitating team, another facilitator should develop the interaction, especially if the participant has become 'hooked into' something a facilitator said or did.

Participation Names – a focus and gathering exercise

Ask participants to reflect on how they participated yesterday and how they need to be in order to strengthen or deepen their participation today. Ask them to think of a name they could give themselves that would define how they will strengthen their participation today, such as '*Listening* Gemma', '*Risk-taking* Raoul', '*Focused* Carlos', '*Unhooked* Aleasia'.

Participants declare their names to the rest of the group and say why they have chosen their particular name.

COMMENTS

Encourage participants to choose names for themselves that move them on in terms of their participation yesterday. If someone finds it hard to think of a name for themselves, you could offer them some observations on how they participated on Day 1. You could also ask for suggestions from the rest of the group about how that person might build on their participation. Let the participant choose for themselves from the suggestions offered to them, so that they take responsibility for their deeper participation.

Fact, Fiction, Faction – a focus and gathering exercise

In a circle, ask participants to relate a *fact* about themselves. The fact can be anything, as long as it is absolutely true.

Then ask participants to relate a *fiction* about themselves. The fiction can be anything, as long as it is a complete lie.

Then ask participants to relate something about themselves which may or may not be true – which could be fact or fiction. For this to work well, participants need to choose something that could be true, or that is a mixture of truth and fiction. For example: 'My father played for Tottenham Hotspurs'. The truth might be that their father had a trial for Spurs; the fiction would be that he actually played for them. This works as a 'faction' because it is unlikely that other participants would know such details about another participant's father.

You can complete a further round where the group guesses which part was fact and which was fiction in each participant's contribution in the 'faction' round.

Feedback

Lead a discussion on the game, relating it to the theme of Acts. You could ask the following questions: 'When do I tell factions? Why do I tell factions or fictions about myself? When do I embellish the truth, so it's not exactly a lie, but no longer the truth? When I am inside an Act, do I know what's me and what's the Act? When does the fiction turn into a "fact"? What is an Act – is it fact, fiction or faction? When do we start to believe the fictions and factions we tell? Do others tell us fictions and factions about ourselves? When do we believe them?'

COMMENTS

If we tell ourselves something often enough, it starts to sound like the truth. Similarly, if others tell us something about ourselves often enough, we begin to believe it. This game can be a lot of fun, and is also a way of recapping on the work done yesterday on Acts and labels.

Focus of the Day

In the past: The history of my Acts – the sentence I created

Day 2 explores the history behind our Acts. Participants will examine how an Act is assembled, and why an Act develops from the past to what it becomes in the present. They will identify key stages on the journey of this development, and examine the thinking and the belief systems that fuel their Acts and keep them inside them. See the introduction to the Advanced Workshop for further comments (pages 98–99).

Discuss the focus and link it to the previous exercise. You could also use the quotes given at the beginning of this section to introduce the Focus of the Day.

Assembling the Act – a large-group discussion

In advance, facilitators should draw six circles as shown in the diagram below. The circles are numbered to help facilitators explain the exercise, and the numbers should not be written onto your diagram. At the centre, surrounded by the six circles, draw a mask.

Show the diagram to the group, explain that the mask represents an Act and that you are going to explore how an Act can be built up over a period of years until it becomes fixed.

- **Circle 1:** Take an example of an Act that has been identified by a number of participants in the group as being familiar. For example, you might take Ms Tough. Ask participants to think of something that might have happened to Ms Tough when she was about five or six years old, that may have caused her to begin to develop that Act. Write one of the most plausible and recognisable suggestions in the first circle (what happened)

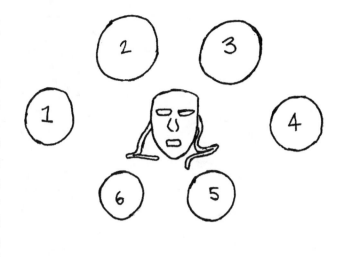

– for example, 'Got hit by mother'. Fill in the circle and label it 'WHAT HAPPENED'.

- **Circles 2 and 3:** Ask participants to imagine what that child might feel and think about what happened. Write up these feelings and thoughts in Circles 2 and 3. The feelings might be 'frightened', 'angry', 'useless'. The thoughts might be 'I'm useless', 'My mother doesn't love me', 'It's all right to hit people'. Label the circles respectively 'THOUGHTS' and 'FEELINGS'.

- **Circle 4:** Ask participants what the child might go on to do following the incident, prompted by its attendant feelings and thoughts. Take one of the suggestions and write it in the fourth circle – for example 'Hit younger brother'. Label the circle 'ACTION'.

- **Circles 5 and 6:** Ask participants to identify possible costs and gains of this action. For example, a gain might be that the child felt better, or less disempowered. Fill in the circles and label them 'COSTS' and 'GAINS'.

- **Mask:** Now shade or colour in a section of the mask. Explain to participants that, for the child, the foundations of the Ms Tough Act are starting to form.

Ask participants to imagine that over the next couple of years this cycle of events continues. Ask them to think of something else that could have happened to Ms Tough, that would provoke her to put another piece of the Act in place. Take participants through the same process as before, using their suggestions to fill in the circles. Continue through four or five cycles of events until Ms Tough is 18 or 19. By this stage the whole of the mask should be coloured in.

Feedback

Lead a discussion using the following questions: 'Where on the circle does Ms Tough feel most powerful? Where on the circle does she feel least powerful? Is there a relationship between feelings of power and powerlessness and the point at which you become your Act? What feelings keep you in your Act? How can you create real power for yourself? Who has the power – you or your Act? Do you control you, or does your Act control you?'

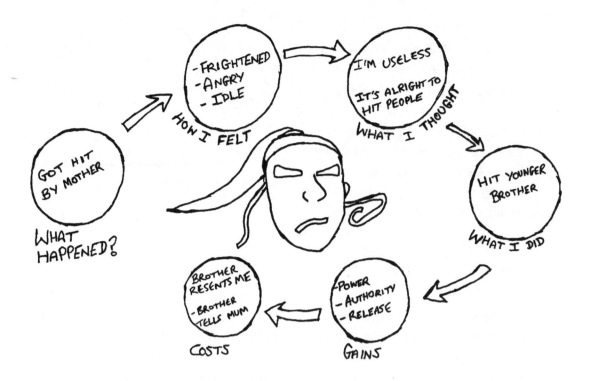

COMMENTS

This exercise deepens the work of 'The Vicious Circle' on Day 3 of the Leadership Workshop (pages 87–90). What keeps someone in their Act is often the feeling of power they gain from it. There is a difference between feelings of power (or powerlessness) and 'being empowered'. Feelings of power or powerlessness can keep someone in their Act. When their Act is in place, they feel *powerful*. When their Act is breached in some way, they feel intensely exposed and *powerless*. This provokes them back into their Act, where they feel powerful again – until the next time when their Act doesn't work.

Alternatively, building and having authentic *personal power* means being able to tolerate feelings of confusion, vulnerability, hurt, anger, etc., without reacting to these feelings and resorting to an Act to mask them.

History of the Act – a freeze-frame exercise in small groups

Ask participants to choose a stock Act that has cost them a lot in their lives. It can be the Act already explored in previous exercises, or a different one.

Ask participants to divide their life into three stages. Ask them to think of a time from each stage when they were inside their Act and it cost them something. Then ask them to think of a picture they could make to represent each of those three different times.

In small groups, ask participants to create three pictures, one for each time they were inside the Act.

Each participant then shares their pictures, beginning with the most recent, with the whole group. Before they begin to share their pictures, ask them to declare the Act whose history they are portraying. For each picture, ask them the following questions:

- How old were you?
- Where are we?
- Who else is in the picture?
- What did it cost you? (Encourage participants to be specific about the cost.)

Feedback

Lead a discussion about the exercise. Some questions you might ask are: 'What was doing that exercise like? What was it like seeing other people's pictures? What is the total cost of your Act in terms of where you are now? Has your Act changed or developed over the years? How? At what age was your Act strongest? How strong is your Act now? When was the very first time you inhabited the Act? How old were you? What was happening in your life that propelled you into the Act?'

COMMENTS

Acts grow stronger, the more we depend on them to get us through life. When we are very young our Acts are just forming, and usually grow out of the meaning we give to a specific happening or circumstance. Sometimes this specific happening or circumstance is quite traumatic in itself, or even indicative of a habitual level of deprivation and abuse. This exercise can provoke powerful memories and emotions in participants, particularly if they identify or share memories from childhood. It is important that the group is ready to do this work, that they have developed sufficient trust in each other, and that they feel confident that what they share will remain within the room. It is equally important that the facilitators are experienced enough to manage this level of work and emotional reaction.

If you have time you can develop this exercise using 'Getting Unhooked' from the Leadership Workshop (pages 81–82). Use the picture of what happened the first time the participant became the Act as the 'Fact' picture. The subsequent translation of this into feelings and thoughts becomes the 'Meaning' picture. The third picture will be of the Act they created. The fourth picture will show the consequences of that Act. This is a powerful way of developing this work on the history of the Act more deeply and will relate directly to work later on in 'Life Sentences' (pages 121–123).

The mood in the group can be quite emotional at the end of this exercise. Participants have shared powerful images and stories with each other. There will be strong connections between participants as they see that they are not alone in some of the things that have happened to them. It is worth reminding participants to take care of themselves and each other over the break, and to ensure that the facilitator team and key staff are available in case anybody wants individual support.

Poster Time

Give participants an adequate opportunity to write up their reflections on this morning's powerful work.

Session 4

Count to Twenty – a group concentration exercise

Participants stand in a circle. The aim of the game is for participants to count from one to 20 out loud, with no-one speaking over others or at the same time. If two participants speak at once, the group goes back to the beginning. Encourage participants not to opt for simple solutions (such as going round the circle, each participant in turn), but instead to concentrate, focus on listening to others, and try to anticipate when others may be about to speak. When they are successful you could ask the group to repeat the exercise with closed eyes.

Feedback

'What did you observe about yourself in this exercise? What did you observe about others? What happened if someone tried to control the game by, for example, indicating to others when to speak? If you controlled the game, why did you do that? What feelings prompted you to do so? When did the game work best? What happened when you gave up trying to control the outcome?'

COMMENTS

Encourage participants to relax. There might be feelings of frustration and impatience if the game takes a while. Encourage participants to note how they are feeling at any given time, but not to become influenced or controlled by their feelings. The game works best when participants give up trying to control the outcome to complete the game as quickly as possible, but instead really focus on being with each other, listening to each other, and trusting that together they will reach 20.

Nine Dots – an exercise to introduce 'Life Sentence'

Draw nine dots in a square, on a piece of flip chart paper:

Ask participants in turn to come forward and draw four straight lines which link all the dots, without taking their pen off the paper and without retracing lines already drawn. Encourage as many participants as possible to have a go.

Feedback

Whether someone in the group provides the solution, or whether you have to provide the solution yourself, ask the following questions: 'What did people try to do at first? What do you have to do to solve the puzzle? Why do you stay inside the box? What is the thinking that keeps you inside the box and prevents you from seeing the solution? What was struggling for the solution like? Did you give up and tell yourself it couldn't be done? If you did this, what happened? Did you go into one of your Acts whilst struggling? Which one?'

COMMENTS

To complete the puzzle, you need to look outside the box formed by the nine dots. This can be difficult to see and do in practise.

To be able to lead a life where the Acts you use do not damage or destroy your life, your friends, your relationships or your future, you need to be able to step outside your Act and examine the core beliefs and thought patterns that keep you inside it. These core beliefs about ourselves keep us locked into a habitual way of behaving in the world. They operate like a 'life sentence' and imprison us inside our Acts.

As with the previous exercise, there may be feelings of frustration and impatience with this game. Encourage participants to notice their reactions but not to be ruled by them. Encourage them to notice the Act they go into when they are working on something that requires them to struggle.

Here is the solution.

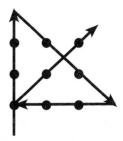

Life Sentence – a small- and large-group discussion exercise

Use the following introduction to link this exercise to the previous one:

> 'Our purpose in this exercise is to look at the core beliefs that fuel our Acts and keep us inside them. Just as we were trapped into a certain way of thinking about the dots that made it hard to find a solution, we also have core beliefs about ourselves and the world that keep us trapped inside our Acts and our habitual behaviour. We are going to discover the core beliefs that keep our Acts in place. These beliefs operate like a life sentence. We can spend our whole lives acting as if these beliefs are true, when in fact they are just things we believe. We could equally well believe something completely different about ourselves, that would let us create more choice and possibility in our lives. This exercise is a continuation of the 'Getting Hooked' exercise that we did in the first workshop. Here, however, we are going to take it to a deeper level, so that we can understand what drives us and begin to create the possibility of exercising choice.'

Use the following example to demonstrate the exercise to the whole group and then split into smaller groups so that each participant can identify their own 'life sentence'.

Remind participants of the three components of 'Getting Hooked': the hook, the line and the sinker. You can use the diagram on the next page as an illustration.

Ask participants for an example of an insult that would 'hook' most people. Write this at 'HOOK'. (A common example is an insult to someone's mother.)

Ask participants to identify the possible thoughts of the person who is hooked. Write these alongside 'LINE OF THOUGHTS'. (In our example the thoughts might be 'This guy's disrespecting my mother', 'Nobody speaks about my mother like that', 'He's disrespecting me', 'He's going to pay for disrespecting me and my family'.) You don't need more than four thoughts to take the exercise on to the next stage.

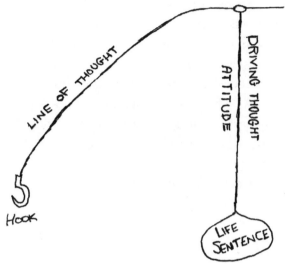

Explain that we are now going to unpack the 'sinker', which holds the thoughts in place. Ask participants to look at the thoughts and identify the *driving thought* or *attitude*. (In our example it might be 'I need respect for me and my family.') Write this along as the line attached to the sinker. Label it 'DRIVING THOUGHT/ ATTITUDE'.

Ask participants to identify the meaning that the hooked person gives to the event of not being shown respect. This usually occurs as an *'if…then…'* statement – for example, 'If you don't show respect to me, then I have no value. Questions that may help identify this statement are: 'What is the belief underneath the attitude? What do you believe about yourself? What do you believe about the world?' Write this statement inside the SINKER and label it 'MEANING'.

The hooked person's 'life sentence' will lie underneath this belief. This will be the sentence or belief that has a profound influence on their attitudes and behaviours. The 'life sentence' consists of a simple statement that encapsulates someone's core belief about themselves or about the world. Here are some examples:

- 'I am worthless.'
- 'I destroy everything.'
- 'The world is a dangerous place.'
- 'I always get it wrong.'
- 'I am valueless.'

Questions to help identify the Life Sentence are: 'What do you *really* believe about yourself? What do you *really* believe about the world? If you really believe you are alright, of value, etc., how do you react when someone challenges it?' When you have identified the life sentence, write it inside the SINKER and label it 'LIFE SENTENCE'.

Divide participants into small groups, each led by a facilitator. Using participants' own examples, take them through a process to unpack their own 'sinkers'. Ask participants to share their discoveries with the whole group.

Feedback

Lead a discussion, using the following questions:

'How has your Life Sentence affected the decisions you have made in your life? How does your Life Sentence affect your interactions? What Acts grew out of that Life Sentence? Where does your Life Sentence come from? How old were you when you sentenced yourself? What was happening? What do you do to disprove or escape your Life Sentence? What do you do to prove or disprove your belief about yourself or your beliefs about the world?

'What if you believed something different about yourself or about the world? How might your life be different? What would become available to you in your life? What possibilities would you be open to? Do you see any connection between your Life Sentence and the work we did this morning on the history of the Act? What connections do you see?'

COMMENTS

Life Sentences are very powerful core beliefs we hold about ourselves or the world. For some of us they are self-fulfilling prophecies. For example, if we believe we are essentially unlovable, then we are likely to have relationships with people who find it hard to love others. When they show that they find it hard to love us, it reinforces our belief about ourselves. If we believe that the world is an unsafe and dangerous place, then we are likely to create situations where this is demonstrated to us, and this reinforces our core belief about the world.

This exercise continues the work of History of the Act in Session 3 (pages 118–119). Usually, our Life Sentence comes directly out of the meaning that we create about ourselves when we are very small, often the same first picture from which our Acts have developed. By identifying their Life Sentence and where it comes from, participants can begin to recognise when they are governed or controlled by it. They can also begin to explore the possibility of what their life might look like without their Life Sentence, and what might then be possible for them.

Poster Time

Give participants an opportunity to write up their reflections on this afternoon's work.

Trust Pictures – a trust exercise in pairs

Ask participants to find a partner and decide between them who is A and who is B.

A is going to create three snapshots for B of objects in the room. B shuts his or her eyes. A then leads B to one of the objects selected and positions B so that B will see what A wants them to see. A then tells B to open and shut his or her eyes, like a shutter on a camera. A continues until three snapshots have been completed by B. Then they swap round.

Feedback

'What was it like to be led? What was it like to lead? What did you see? Did you see anything in a way you hadn't seen it before? Did you see anything you didn't expect to see? What was it like having someone else determine what you see? How much freedom do you have in the way you see things usually? How much freedom do you have in the way you view friends, relationships, situations, opportunities, etc.? Do you control the way you see, or does your Life Sentence control the way you see? How does your Life Sentence affect the way you see things?'

COMMENTS

Our Life Sentence is the filter through which we view the world. Looking at life through the filter of our Life Sentence is like looking at the world through blinkers. What we are looking and listening for is, for example, 'unloveable', or 'worthless', and we are closed to seeing or hearing anything else. You could develop this exercise by asking participants to identify situations that they have viewed through the blinkers of their Life Sentence and consider how different it might have looked if viewed through a different lens.

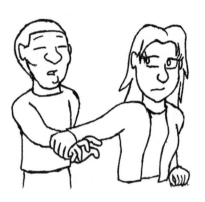

Closing – a large-group reflection and feedback exercise

Ask each participant to comment honestly on their level of participation today. When were the moments that they checked out, switched off, felt bored or irritated? When were the moments when they went into an Act? Encourage participants to reflect on their participation without judgement, but rather as an inquiry into their own habits of attention and inattention.

FINAL COMMENTS ON THE DAY

In this workshop, far more than in the previous workshop, the spotlight is really on the individual participants. All of their behaviour is up for scrutiny and possible challenge in terms of it being an Act. Expect a real variety in responses and feedback at the end of the day. Some participants may be exhausted and confused and still defending, or stuck inside, their Acts. Others may be feeling quite light and exhilarated and will have achieved some useful insights and understandings for themselves. This range of responses is normal.

Remind participants of 'Count to Twenty' or 'Nine Dots', and how the level of frustration and struggle was most intense just before a solution was found. At the moment you are only two-thirds of the way through the workshop, or two-thirds of the way through the puzzle, and that is often when the struggle is hardest. Reassure them that tomorrow will help them make more sense of the past two days, and begin to provide them with a way out of the puzzle of their Acts and Life Sentence. Affirm everyone's participation, tell them to get a good night's rest and remind them that Day 3 will start with a clearing.

If someone has a lot of front they usually have a lot of back too.

Course participant

Who am I if I am not my Act?

Course participant

Day 3
Focus: *For the future*

Giving up the Act – choosing who I am

Agenda

Session 5

- Clearing
- Empty Chair
- Focus of the Day
- Under the Act
- Roots of Anger
- Poster Time
- Trust Conveyor

Session 6

- Giving Up the Act
- Personal Destroyers
- Sharing Posters
- Acknowledgements
- Evaluation
- The Next Step
- Closing Ceremony

QUOTES TO INTRODUCE THE DAY

One half of knowing what you want is knowing what you must give up before you get it.

Sidney Howard

It's not whether you get knocked down.
It's whether you get up again.

Vince Lombardi

The chief cause of pain and unhappiness is giving up what we want the most for what we want in the moment.

Anon

Session 5

Clearing – a reflection exercise on the previous day

Begin the day in the same way as Day 2, with a short clearing (see page 115 for instructions).

Empty Chair – a warm-up game

You will need a chair for each participant. Place the chairs randomly about the room. Ask for a volunteer to begin the game. All the other participants sit on a chair, leaving one chair empty. The volunteer stands as far away from the empty chair as possible. When the game begins, their aim is to occupy a chair. As they walk towards the empty chair, other participants move to occupy it, leaving other chairs empty – which they then move to occupy. All the while the volunteer is trying to occupy a chair.

When the volunteer gets a chair, the person who was last on that chair becomes the next volunteer, and the game begins again.

Feedback

Lead a discussion about the game, using the following questions: 'What happens to the empty chair? As you are aiming for the empty chair, what happens to it? What is it like, always rushing after the empty chair? Did anybody draw any meaning from rushing to fill the chair, or about the chair being empty? Did anybody draw any meaning from not getting a chair quickly enough, or being caught out?'

COMMENTS

The empty chair always gets filled up, just as in life we get filled up with our Acts, our Life Sentence, our meanings about what has happened to us. If we believe that life has no meaning in itself and that *we* create the meaning, then everything becomes possible. Stepping free of your Life Sentence and giving up your Acts makes it possible to choose what you make your life mean.

Focus of the Day

For the future: Giving up the Act – choosing who I am

Day 3 aims to create a way of being in the world which is not constrained by the meanings we give events and happenings, our Acts or our Life Sentences.

Participants will be introduced to a powerful tool to communicate the feelings that are often hidden under their Acts. They will give and receive support from their peers. They will also practise giving up an Act when faced with a challenge that would normally bring it to life.

You could use the 'Empty Chair' exercise as a way to introduce the Focus of the Day.

Under the Act – a freeze-frame exercise in small groups to prepare for 'Roots of Anger'

Ask participants to choose one of their Acts to work on. They may wish to choose an Act that they have not yet explored in the workshop.

Divide participants into threes. Ask them to make a picture of the Act and, behind the picture, two more pictures that each represent a feeling masked by the Act, or which is buried somewhere inside the Act. Each participant represents their own Act and then sculpts one of the other two participants into the feeling masked by the Act. They then sculpt the other participant into an image of the feeling that lies even deeper, beneath the first feeling. Each participant should end up with a series of three figures: the first figure represents their Act, the second the feeling masked by the Act, and the third figure the deeper feeling underneath the first one.

Ask participants to give each of their figures a one-word title. For example, someone working with their 'Ms Tough' Act might have Ms Tough as their first picture, and two others, entitled 'Angry' and 'Frightened' as their first and second feelings respectively.

Share the pictures with the whole group. Ask for volunteers to step in and assume the first Act picture each time, so that the participant who is sharing can step back and see their own pictures from outside the tableau. Ask the following questions of each participant as they share their pictures: 'What act are we seeing? What are the titles for your feeling pictures?'

Feedback

When everyone has shared their pictures, lead a discussion, using the following questions: 'What was it like seeing those pictures? Did any of the pictures surprise you? How did you feel, sharing your pictures with others? How easy was it to identify the feelings underneath the Act? How easy was it to identify the deeper feeling in the third picture? How often do you share your feelings? Who do you talk to? How do you talk about your feelings? For how long can you talk about your real feelings? Do you find that some feelings are harder to acknowledge than others? Which ones? Why? Do you have your feelings or do your feelings have you?'

COMMENTS

This exercise prepares participants for a more in depth exploration of feelings in the next exercise, 'Roots of Anger'. It may be hard for participants to find the third picture, the one representing deeper feelings. They may access this picture more easily if you encourage them to work with the images first and give them titles afterwards, rather than thinking of the feelings and then making a picture of them.

Encourage participants to use a word that describes the feeling specifically, rather than one that is more general. For example, the word 'upset' could describe a range of different feelings, while it is clear what words like 'irritated' or 'angry' describe. Developing a vocabulary to describe our emotions helps us to gain more control over ourselves when we are experiencing strong emotions. Learning to recognise and identify specific feelings helps us communicate them accurately to others.

Roots of Anger – an explorative exercise in communication

Ask participants to think about a time in their life when they felt angry about something or with someone and, instead of speaking about their anger, went into an Act. Ask them to state what they were angry about in one clear sentence – for example: 'I was angry with my father because he did not keep his word to me.'

Divide the participants into pairs. Ask them to focus on this situation, and to complete the following three statements about it. They then share the sentences with their partner:

It **hurts** me because…

For example: 'It hurts me because I feel let down and I can't trust my own father.'

What I **need** is….

For example: 'What I need is someone whom I can trust in my life, someone whom I can rely on.'

I **fear** that…

For example: 'I fear that I will never have someone like that in my life.'

Once the participants have completed all statements, they can share their complete example with the rest of the group. In many cases they will need help to make their statements clear and precise, in one short sentence. Pay particular attention to the statement dealing with needs. A personal/emotional need should be expressed, and not a desire for action – not, for example, 'I need my father to change,' or 'I need my father to get out of my life for good.' The need should be focused within the speaker.

Participants who struggle to create all four statements can get ideas from listening to other examples from the group.

By the end of this exercise, each participant should have created four clear statements about one situation where they have experienced anger.

Ask participants to think of a time when they faced the anger of someone else. Ask them to repeat this exercise as if they were the other person, imagining the source of the other person's anger. Get them to share some examples in the group.

Feedback

Some suggestions for feedback questions are: 'What have you learnt about yourself from doing this exercise? What was it like discovering for yourself what lies underneath your anger? What was it like sharing this with others? What benefit could this have for you in your life? In what ways can this exercise support you to deal with your own anger? How would it feel to speak from one of the underlying feelings rather than from the anger? How comfortable would you find this? How much of a risk would it be for you? In what ways can this exercise support you in giving up your Acts? How could you use this knowledge when facing the anger of another person? What have you learnt about others in this exercise? What have you learnt about Acts? In what ways can this exercise support you when dealing with the anger of others? How can it support you when dealing with others' Acts?'

COMMENTS

The exercise explores what lies beneath an expression of anger. We often communicate only our anger, and do not acknowledge (even to ourselves) what lies beneath. This exercise helps participants focus on what *underlies* their anger; a sense of hurt, a basic need they experience, a fear they have. It works to identify these elements and help participants communicate them clearly to others.

The aim in this exercise is to extend the participants' range and level of communication, to enable them go beyond what they would normally be prepared to share with others, and to fully acknowledge for themselves their feelings and emotions. Encourage them to explore a situation that really matters to them, and where they really want to create a deeper understanding of their reaction and their retreat into an Act. This exercise can create a powerful sense of sharing and communication in the room.

Poster Time

Give everyone an opportunity to write up their reflections on the last exercise.

Trust Conveyor – a trust exercise

This exercise works best with a larger group of participants. Ask for a volunteer to begin this exercise. The rest of the group stand shoulder to shoulder in two straight lines facing each other at arm's length. Participants should stand opposite someone of roughly similar height. The volunteer lies on the floor at the beginning of the 'conveyor' with their arms folded across their chest and their eyes closed.

The participants standing on either side place their hands underneath the volunteer and, when the facilitator says 'go', raise the volunteer to waist height and then to shoulder height. Make sure that participants bend their knees and use their legs rather than their backs when lifting. Participants need to work together to pass the person slowly and gently down the conveyor until the end where they are lowered carefully to the ground.

Repeat the exercise until everyone who wants to has been lifted and passed along the line. If you feel confident that the group is working well together, you can delegate the giving of instructions to a participant.

COMMENTS

This exercise is an effective way of building cooperation and teamwork within the group in preparation for the afternoon's work. Encourage participants to create a sense of calm and safety in the way that they hold and lift each other. They have created a sense of emotional trust in each other through the three days of the workshop so far, and this exercise marks the high level of physical trust they have developed by this stage.

Session 6

Giving Up the Act – a gathering and focusing exercise in preparation for 'Personal Destroyers'

Ask participants to think about their future. What would their life be like if they lifted their Life Sentence and gave up their Acts? What do they hope for themselves? What could they achieve in their lives?

Each participant gets a chance to respond to this. If their responses are brief, ask support questions to get more information. For example, if a participant says they would be happier, ask them what would be making them happy, who else would be there, where they would be living, etc.

Then ask participants what might stop them achieving their goals? What are the events and circumstances that might prevent them? What would be the event or circumstance that could put them back under their Life Sentence and inside their Acts? Ask participants to identify the Act that is *most likely* to stop them achieving their goals.

Ask participants to share their responses to the last two questions with the whole group. Then ask for a volunteer who would like an opportunity to work on overcoming their Act.

Personal Destroyers – a structured role-play exercise

For this exercise you need a volunteer with a clearly defined Act which will get in the way of them achieving their goal, as identified in the previous exercise. Other participants will play supporting parts. Use labels or stickers to indicate the various roles other participants will take on during this exercise.

A representative scenario might be:

> *Hope for the Future*: 'I want to go to college and get my qualifications.'
>
> *What could stop me*: 'Losing my temper and ending up inside again.'
>
> *Personal Destroyer Act*: Mr Hard Man.

This exercise is like the 'Boxing Ring' in the Leadership Workshop (see pages 91–93) in that it involves a *challenger* versus an *opponent* and is run in rounds like a boxing match. This time, however, the challenger is going into the ring opposite one of their own Acts. The opponent

is going to play this Personal Destroyer Act, so they need to understand it and how it operates. The opponent's job is to try to talk the challenger into adopting or inhabiting the Act. The opponent needs to know the kind of things the Personal Destroyer says and does in order to provoke the challenger. The challenger's job is to find a way of dealing with this Act and not slip into being controlled by it. The challenger identifies a situation where they would normally slip into the Act; this will

give focus to the dialogue with that Act. In the example given above a particular insult might be enough to provoke a challenger to adopt Mr Hard Man, their Personal Destroyer Act.

Ask for two volunteers to act as *coaches* in the challenger's corner. Their task is to support the challenger during the breaks between rounds, provide positive feedback on how they are doing, whether or not they are slipping into their Act, and to talk to them in ways that acknowledge their Personal Destroyer Act but keep them from slipping into it.

Ask for two volunteers to act as *coaches* for the opponent's corner. Their task is to give opponents feedback on whether they are getting through, and ideas and strategies to lure the challenger into slipping into their Personal Destroyer Act.

Ask for a volunteer to play the *personal trainer*. Their task is to sit in the ring near the challenger and give specific coaching *when requested by the challenger*. The personal trainer joins the challenger in their coaching corner between rounds, but unlike the other coaches can also contribute coaching whilst the challenger is in the ring. However, they can only contribute when the challenger specifically asks for it.

Other participants can be *observers* to the two corners. Their task is to observe how well the challenger stays out of an Act. They need to be aware not only of the Act that the challenger is tackling in the ring, but also of other Acts that the challenger may slip into. They may need to be reminded of the challenger's stock Acts identified on Day 1. Observers do not participate during the rounds or breaks, and must wait until the end to give their comments.

The facilitator plays the role of *referee*. They mark out an area with chairs in which the role-play will take place, and they call the beginning and end of each round. If the challenger is having too hard a time, the referee should end the round and return the challenger to their corner for some coaching. If the challenger is succeeding too easily, the referee ends the round so that the opponent playing the Personal Destroyer Act can receive some coaching. The referee consults with the challenger's corner to determine how the challenger is doing, and how long the next round should be. The referee tells all the participants when the last round is being called.

The challenger can tell the Personal Destroyer Act to 'Be quiet' in any round. This means that the opponent has to shut up for 30 seconds and hear the challenger out. After 30 seconds, however, the opponent can begin to speak again. When the challenger asks their personal trainer for coaching, their trainer can remind them of the 'Be quiet' rule.

The referee can at any time call a *freeze* to the action to give an instruction. Similarly the challenger can call a *time-out* and the referee will end the round. The coaches can also indicate to the referee if they feel the challenger needs support from their corner.

All participants should remember that their ultimate aim is to support the challenger, helping them to gain the confidence and skills necessary to overcome their Personal Destroyer Act.

At the end of the role-play, welcome the role-players back as themselves, and give each role-player an opportunity to say how they felt playing the role and to speak to their role. One way of doing this is to ask each of them to remove their role-play sticker, stick it on the chair or the wall and ask if there is anything they would like to say to their role. Make sure you de-role the challenger, the opponent, the coaches for both corners and the personal trainer.

Feedback

Bring the group together and ask each participant to mention a skill or a quality they saw being used effectively during the exercise. Ask the players to give specific feedback to their coaches about what worked well for them; ask the coaches for specific feedback to the players on what they did well. Keep the feedback positive and focused on what participants did well at this stage.

Then lead a discussion about the exercise using the following questions: What coaching worked well in this exercise? What coaching didn't work well? What tactics were successful? What tactics weren't successful? How easy is it to receive support when you are in a challenging situation? How did the challenger make use of their personal trainer? How did they make use of the 'Be quiet' rule? What happened when the challenger used the 'Be quiet' rule? What was it like when the Personal Destroyer Act was silent? How would it be not to have your that voice loud in your ear? What happened when the challenger tried to argue or fight with the Personal Destroyer Act? What other Acts did you see the challenger slipping into?

COMMENTS

It is important that the challenger has a Personal Destroyer Act clearly defined for themselves and a specific situation in which they habitually slip into this Act. The opponent needs a good understanding of both the situation and the Act.

In the heat of the exercise the challenger's corner often forgets the 'Be quiet' rule so you may need to remind them of this tool. The Personal Destroyer Act being silent often provokes confusion in the challenger. We are not used to silence from our Acts. We are used to hearing their voices inside our heads at all times and the challenger may be uncertain how to fill the silence when their Act falls silent. Encourage them to allow themselves to experience their Personal Destroyer Act being silent, without filling that silence with another Act. You may need to alert the challenger if they are slipping into another Act.

The best kind of coaching for the challenger will come from coaches who are not inside their own Acts and who have not slipped into becoming sidekicks to the challenger's Acts. You may need to point out to the challenger's coaches that they are getting hooked into trying to destroy the Personal Destroyer Act, rather than helping the challenger to create choice for themselves. Encourage the coaches to stay unhooked and to give specific, clear coaching, such as 'Speak about how you feel', or 'Use the "Be quiet" Rule.'

The challenger's corner may often try to fight the Act, to get it to shut up, remove itself or even leave the room! In life this is not possible. Our Acts will always be with us, but we can learn to control how loudly they talk to us and how much we listen to them and are influenced by them. We need to learn how to transform them from Personal Destroyers into thoughts and feelings that we can recognise and govern, rather than being governed by them. It is important to remember the learning from the previous two days: Acts often come from a place of deep hurt. Sometimes the most powerful tool the challenger can use towards their Personal Destroyer Act is an expression of compassion, such as 'I know how hurt you've been in the past.'

As the referee you need to be aware of what is happening in both corners, in terms of the coaching the challenger and opponent are receiving, and how the challenger is feeling. Use the time during the breaks between rounds to assess how the two corners are doing. (If there are two facilitators it is sometimes useful for one of the facilitators to join a coaching corner and offer occasional support and guidance to the coaches if they are struggling.)

The best outcome for this exercise is when the challenger moves from fighting their Personal Destroyer Act to being able both to hear what the Personal Destroyer is saying and to communicate in an assertive and compassionate manner their intention to transform their relationship with their Act. In the end, we hand over power to our Acts and our Life Sentences, and only we can choose to see them as just thoughts, feelings and perceptions that we can be led by or otherwise disregard.

Sharing Posters – a personal reflection exercise as part of completing the workshop

Ask participants to spend some time reading their posters and adding any final comments.

Ask them to remove their posters from the wall and then to share them with a partner. Ask them to share also a personal challenge they have achieved for themselves during the workshop, something they have discovered about themselves, and something they will be taking away with them.

Participants can then choose to share some of what they have discussed in their pairs with the large group.

Acknowledgements – a group personal feedback exercise as part of completing the workshop

The whole group stands in a circle. Select a participant and ask them to stand in the centre of the circle. Ask for an acknowledgement for them from three members of the group. The participant then receives three acknowledgements. They do not reply – they just listen to what is being said. This gives participants an opportunity to be appreciated for the way in which they participated, for the support that they gave to others or the group, for a quality that was noticed, or for something that was admired about them.

When the participant has received the acknowledgements, they receive a round of applause from the group and step out of the centre of the circle, and the next participant steps in to receive their acknowledgements.

Evaluation – a feedback exercise as part of completing the workshop

It is important that participants have an opportunity to give the facilitators feedback on the strengths and weaknesses of the Advanced Leadership Workshop. See page 95 for ideas on how to evaluate the workshop.

The Next Step – giving information and gathering ideas

Facilitators can give information on the opportunities available for participants to continue this training and to practise and develop their ideas. This might be an opportunity to talk about the 'Fear and Fashion' or Leadership in Action workshops, as well as further leadership opportunities in the programme.

Closing Ceremony – a completion of the workshop

See page 95 for ideas on how to close the workshop.

FINAL COMMENTS ON THE DAY

This three-day workshop can be a very intense experience for everyone!

Participants are struggling to understand new concepts and frameworks that are being offered to them, at the same time as being asked to reflect on their behaviour and long-held beliefs and perceptions. This is tough work for participants, and it is important that facilitators are sensitive in gauging how much of a challenge a particular participant can tolerate. Some participants will need or want to return to this workshop again. The material from this workshop can be returned to, developed and expanded in any follow-up and/or support sessions with participants, on either a one-to-one or a group basis.

This can also be an exhilarating, exhausting and challenging rollercoaster ride of a workshop for facilitators! As you go through the course, your own learning about your own Acts and Life Sentence will be reactivated by your engagement with this content. For that reason it is preferable that you have experienced this workshop as a participant before you attempt to facilitate it. Your experience of the process will help you to provide the very best opportunity for participants to engage as deeply as possible with the material. Sharing authentically but carefully with participants some edited examples of your own struggle with Acts or Life Sentence, at appropriate moments in the workshop, may help them unlock the doors to their own understanding and reassure them that what they are dealing with is universal human behaviour.

As with the Leadership Workshop, you need to accept that participants will get what they get at the time from the workshop, and that you too will get what you get at the time. Everyone will gain different insights and achieve different levels of change or understanding. We find that, very often, further insights and understandings emerge at a later time for some individuals. What you can do is provide the very best opportunity, support and conditions for them to participate. You may want to remind participants that, although this particular workshop has now ended, their learning about themselves and how to create their life, rather than have life create them, continues throughout the remainder of the Leadership Programme.

Life is not a having and a getting,
but a being and a becoming.

Matthew Arnold

The truth is like gold:
keep it locked up,
and you will find it exactly as you first put it away.

from Senegal

Chapter 8
The Leadership in Action Workshop

Introduction to the Leadership in Action Workshop

This three-day Leadership in Action Workshop is intended for participants who want to apply what they have learnt in the previous workshops in a community environment, making a direct contribution to the well-being of others by taking on a leadership role.

The workshop focus

This workshop focuses on listening, communicating, supporting, acknowledging and facilitating. While the Leadership Workshop and the Advanced Leadership Workshop encourage participants to turn *inwards* to focus on themselves and their own feelings, thoughts, attitudes and behaviours, this workshop encourages them to turn *outwards* and focus on the power and influence they can have with others. Ideally, the Leadership in Action Workshop should be made available to all those who have completed the first two Leadership Workshops successfully.

- **Day 1** explores issues of leadership and power, and the importance of giving and receiving support.

- **Day 2** focuses on how to apply the insights participants have gained, not only to their own lives, but also to working with people and contributing to the well-being of others. We look at how to work creatively with conflict and acknowledge our mistakes.

- **Day 3** concentrates on taking the lead and building community. We focus on the specific facilitation skills needed to be able to deliver peer education and training workshops to others, and to run small-group work with peers.

This chapter simply provides an outline for the Leadership in Action Workshop, rather than the full details given in the previous Leadership Workshops. The facilitation methods, exercises, feedbacks, discussions and games used are all very similar to those in the first two workshops. This outline is intended as a guide to those developing this process, and highlights key areas and techniques that have been relevant and useful in the past. This workshop should be facilitated by staff who have built up confidence and experience with the Leadership Workshops, as this will give them a natural feel for what it is that their particular young people need if they are to play a leadership role.

If young people are training as peer trainers and facilitators, they will need opportunities to practise delivering the content of the workshops that they will be leading for their peers. Some of the material contained in the other three workshops can be adapted for teams of peer trainers to deliver, and should be selected according to the specific aims of the peer training workshops. For example, if peer trainers are going to deliver workshops on conflict awareness, they might practise delivering 'Red flags' from Chapter 6. If they are delivering workshops on knife awareness and prevention, they might practise delivering 'Where Do You Stand?' from Chapter 9. These practice sessions could be substituted for activities on Days 2 and 3 of the Leadership in Action Workshop.

Day 1

Focus: *Developing yourself as a resource*

Leadership and power – giving and receiving support

Agenda

- Gathering
- Introduction to the Workshop
- Trust Walk
- Focus of the Day
- Power Relations
- Power Game
- Triangle of Support
- Games
- In Someone Else's Shoes
- Closing

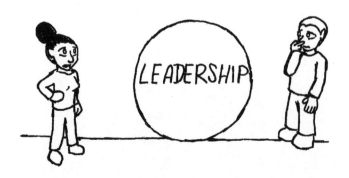

Quotes to Introduce the Day

If you only do things you know well and do comfortably, you'll never reach higher goals.

Linda Tsao Yang

Nothing is so strong as real gentleness,
nothing is so gentle as real strength.
Greatness lies not in being strong,
but in the right use of strength.

Anon

Gathering – a focusing exercise

This exercise aims to focus all the participants, to reconnect them with the experience they had last time, and to enable them to share some of the expectations or reservations they might now have. Each participant should be given a chance to introduce themselves and respond to these questions:

- How did you feel when leaving the last workshop?
- How do you feel coming back into this workshop today?
- What do you expect from this Leadership in Action Workshop?

Introduction to the Workshop

This introduction should cover the same points as suggested in the other Leadership Workshops (see pages 57–58 and 97–99). However, the focus and the intention of this workshop is obviously different. When introducing this workshop, it is a good idea to remind participants of the intention and aims that were shared in the others. This is best done by asking them to explain what they actually did and achieved in the last workshop. Congratulate them on volunteering for this workshop, and affirm them for taking leadership and choosing to make a contribution to others.

Group guidelines

See the Advanced Workshop for suggestions on how to develop guidelines around behaviour with the group (see pages 98–100).

Trust Walk – a trust exercise in pairs

A trust exercise is recommended for each day of this workshop. The three exercises in this workshop build on the trust exercises done in the last one, but provide more of a challenge.

Ask each participant to think of a favourite place, a special place they would love to visit. It is a place full of fond memories, a place where they might feel at peace, happy, or relaxed.

Divide the group into pairs. Each participant now gets a chance to take their partner on a visit to this favourite place. The partner closes their eyes. Each person leads their partner on a journey to and around their favourite place, describing it to them as they walk and sharing with them what is special about that particular place.

The person leading the Trust Walk is responsible for the safety of their partner. They should handle and lead their partner in such a way that they can relax and enjoy the experience.

When the first 'visit' is complete, give the pairs a chance to discuss the 'journey' they have just undertaken. They then swap over and repeat the process.

Feedback

The participants could share about the kind of places they chose. They could also reflect on what those places mean to them, and 'give' them. They could share what it was like to take someone else to their favourite place. They could reflect on what it was like to be taken on a 'visit' to someone else's special place. They could describe the way in which their partner communicated with them and led them through the experience.

COMMENTS

The mental image that participants build of their favourite place, brought vividly alive in this exercise by describing it to their partner, could be something they use to centre themselves in the future, to calm themselves at a difficult time, or to uplift themselves.

This exercise encourages them to share and to communicate in an interesting and imaginative way with others. It encourages them to be generous, to give something of themselves, and to take care of someone else; and conversely, to be willing to take interest in another person's life and feelings, nurturing empathy. It encourages them to take charge and give someone else a worthwhile experience. These are all qualities and skills we wish to promote in this workshop.

Focus of the Day

Developing yourself as a resource: Leadership and power – giving and receiving support

This should be linked to the discussion after the Trust Walk.

Discuss leadership in terms of:

- contributing to others, giving support, and being generous
- always being prepared to go one step beyond where you would normally stop; this is crucial when providing leadership and motivation for others to extend themselves and live up to their full potential
- a leader can only inspire others if they themselves are inspired
- a leader can only give others courage if they themselves have courage.

This is a 'walk the walk' and 'do as I do' programme, always leading by example.

You can use some of the quotes on page 139 in this discussion.

Power Relations – a warm-up exercise using freeze-frame technique

Working in pairs, participants sculpt themselves into frozen positions, so that one of them has power and the other none, or less power. They then swap over and create another still picture, with the roles reversed. All the pictures are shared with the whole group.

Try the same routine in groups of three, with the third person trying to intervene between the other two who are in a power relationship with each other. Share these pictures with the whole group.

Feedback

Some questions to use are: 'How would you describe someone displaying such power over another? What would you call such a person? Think about the types of behaviour that were shown by those in weaker positions. How would you describe them? What would you call them? How would you characterise the behaviour of the person who intervened? What would you call these people?'

COMMENT

In the 'Power Relations' game, and the 'Power Game' that follows, we begin to introduce an understanding and awareness around the subject of power. We explore different kinds of power, how it can be used and abused, the relationship different individuals might have with it, and how it relates to taking leadership. In preparing participants to take the lead with their peers it essential they reach some clarity as to where power originates and sits, and around the use of power. This exercise continues and deepens the discussion about Power that was initiated in 'Assembling the Act' on Day 2 of the Advanced Workshop (See pages 116–118).

Power Game – a personal reflection exercise using freeze-frame technique

This Power Game focuses on three types of behaviour:

- the **bully**, who intimidates, blames, insults and persecutes others
- the **victim**, who blames themselves, feels sorry for themselves and sees themselves as the victim
- the **do-gooder**, who feels pity for the victim, and always wants to help them or rescue them but doesn't encourage the victim to help themselves. The do-gooder needs victims in order to feel good about him/herself.

These three behaviours are all interrelated and none can function without the other two. They are all part of a power game, in that the players have no real power outside of their specific relationships. In other words, they only have positional power. None is interested in empowering themselves or any of the others. They are trapped in destructive relationships. The aim here is for participants to gain greater self-awareness by understanding the particular dynamics involved in these three ways of behaving and recognising what can happen when they take on one of these roles.

Divide participants into small groups. Ask them each to create a frozen picture showing a time in their life when they behaved in any one of the above three ways. Challenge them to find a personal example of all three of these behaviours for themselves, even if they do not share all of them.

These pictures should be shared with the whole group. Ask the group to identify the gains of each behaviour for the individual – for example, 'I always get what I want' – as well as the costs of the behaviour – for example, 'It is never my fault so I don't get to be responsible for my actions.' Ask them to identify what need each role is satisfying – for example, 'I need to feel important and powerful' or 'I need to be wanted and liked.'

Feedback

Refer participants back to themes used in the previous two workshops, such as the work on Acts. Indeed, the three roles described above are like Acts that people fall into in particular situations.

Some possible questions are: 'Which one of the three behaviours was most familiar to you, whether you recognised it in yourself or in others? What difficulties could you have if you behave in one of these three ways when you are in a leadership role? How would it be difficult for you to lead someone who was behaving in one of these three ways? In what ways are the above-mentioned behaviours part of an Act? What would it be like to give up one of these Acts? What would become available to you if you gave up one of these Acts?

'Can you be an empowering leader if you are inside your Mr Hard Man Act, your Ms Angry Act, or your Poor Me Act? What is difficult in breaking out of a set pattern of behaviour? What would stop you breaking out of a particular role you have been playing? How would you describe taking leadership as a behaviour? How does it compare with the types of behaviour we have been exploring?'

COMMENTS

Encourage the group to clarify the kind of behaviour that leadership calls forth. They now have three very distinct behaviours against which to contrast leadership. It is important that they be able to identify leadership as a role that *empowers*, in contrast to the disempowering function of the other behaviours. It is important that they recognise empowerment as the development of personal power *for themselves and for others*. The primary purpose of giving and receiving support, which is explored in the next exercise, is to develop this kind of power within themselves and others.

It is important to create the distinction between someone who habitually adopts victim-like behaviour, and someone who is a genuine victim of bullying or violence.

Triangle of Support – a personal sharing exercise

The three roles played in 'Power Game' exist inside a triangle that is oppressive to all three. This exercise aims to create another triangle that supports its participants – one in which all three parties are committed to supporting themselves and each other. The three kinds of support that complete the triangle are: receiving support, supporting oneself, and giving support to others.

The way the participants relate to all kinds of support is crucial to their development as resourceful leaders. The aim in this workshop is to transform participants' relationship to giving, as well as receiving, support. The first person that leaders need to support is themselves.

Divide the participants into pairs or in small groups, and ask them to share experiences that they have had around support.

Suggestions for questions to focus on are: 'When did you ask for support and not receive it? When were you asked to give support and didn't give it? When did you need support and not ask for it? When did you offer support and it was not accepted? When did you give up asking for support? When did you give up offering support to others? When did you give support to yourself? When did you not give support to yourself? When did you give up on supporting yourself? What would it take for you to allow yourself to be supported by others? What would it take for you to be available to give support to others?'

Alternatively, participants could create freeze-frame images showing experiences they have had around support, and then discuss the questions above.

COMMENTS

The group now has an understanding of the key role that support plays in personal development. They can appreciate the difference between supporting someone and intimidating, bullying, forcing, dominating, helping, rescuing or saving them.

Games

We recommend including at least one or two games per day in this workshop. They are particularly useful when you need to raise the energy, refocus the group, or when the participants would welcome a chance to relax or to let off steam. You could repeat games that participants enjoyed from the first two workshops, or introduce new games.

In Someone Else's Shoes – a group personal support exercise

Ask each participant to write down on a small index card a dilemma, a conflict, an upset or a problem that they are struggling with in their lives. They write just a brief synopsis of what is at the heart of their personal struggle.

An example could be, 'I have been unfaithful to my boyfriend. I feel he will soon find out. It is better if he finds out from me. I am scared of what his reaction will be. I don't want to lose him. I don't know what to do.'

Another example could be, 'I have been stealing money from my mother. I want to tell her. I want to apologise to her. I know she will kick me out of the house. I don't want that. Maybe it is better not to tell her.'

Collect the cards, shuffle them and redistribute them amongst the group, so that everyone has a new card and nobody has their original one. One option is for the facilitators to write out each dilemma on a card in their own handwriting to ensure that the topics remain anonymous and confidential.

Each participant reads the problem on the card they have, and thinks about what they would do in such circumstances. They share their 'solution' with the group. Other group members can give a brief input if they think they would do something different.

If the person whose dilemma is being discussed wants to, they can respond to the suggestions. They might have further questions on the same subject that they would like to ask the group. This part of the process is purely voluntary. Some participants might prefer to listen in silence to the suggestions about their dilemma, and not to disclose themselves or say anything in response. They should know that this is absolutely alright.

Feedback

'What kind of suggestions were useful or effective? What kind of suggestions were not useful or effective? What do we gain from sharing a dilemma with others? What do we gain by hearing different suggestions as to how other people would handle our situation? What was your experience of receiving support from others in this exercise? What was your experience of giving support to someone else in this exercise? What was your experience of supporting yourself in this exercise? What did you learn from listening to other people's situations and to the suggestions made to resolve them? What support does a leader need? How can a leader encourage someone else to ask for support?'

COMMENTS

Just by contributing to this exercise, by sharing a dilemma, and by being open to suggestions, participants have taken a big step in supporting themselves. It is important, when they respond to someone else's dilemma, that they just give their own personal response to how they would handle the situation. They really work to put themselves into the shoes of the person experiencing the dilemma. Do not allow participants who are making contributions to take on the role of giving advice, lecturing, or counselling. They are only to share their response, for what it is worth. The listener then is free to use the ideas that they like or find useful.

The focus in this exercise is to build trust and openness, to encourage participants to be vulnerable, and to practise giving and receiving support. The environment needs to be non-threatening and non-judgemental.

Allowing group members the freedom to remain anonymous if they prefer will encourage them to participate and allow them to share things that might be difficult. The eventual aim is for them to be confident in this support process, and eventually to reach a stage when they can read out their own dilemma to the group and invite a response.

Leaders need the courage to share themselves and, in so doing, encourage others to do the same. Leaders need to be able both to ask for support and to allow people to give them support, and in this way to encourage others to ask for support for themselves as well.

Closing – a large-group reflection and feedback exercise

In closing, the participants could be asked to reflect on the questions:

- What have I discovered about support today?
- What have I discovered about myself today?

This is also an opportunity for participants to say anything they need to express before leaving the workshop.

FINAL COMMENTS ON THE DAY

As on the first day in both of the previous two workshops, our aim is to recreate the group, bring the participants back into this particular learning environment, and to further the leadership training process. At this stage the participants are taking part not just to develop themselves, but are conscious of doing so with the specific additional purpose of making a contribution to the well-being of others.

We lift ourselves by our thought,
we climb upon our vision of ourselves.

Orison Swett Marden

Obstacles are those frightful things we see
when we take our eyes off the goal.

Hannah More

Day 2

Focus: *Working with others*

Working creatively with conflict – acknowledging mistakes

Agenda

- Gathering
- Trust Fall
- Focus of the Day
- Building a Tower
- Three-Two-One
- Game
- Playing with Fire
- Support Yourself
- Closing

QUOTES TO INTRODUCE THE DAY

Do what you can, with what you have,
where you are.

Theodore Roosevelt

We should concentrate more on constructive self-
criticism and on frankly and publicly acknowledging
our own mistakes to our own people. Far from being
a sign of weakness, it is a measure of one's strength
and confidence, which will pay dividends in the end.

*Nelson Mandela, unpublished sequel to his autobiography,
circa 1998*

We tell our your leaders:
'Don't be afraid to make a mistake,
but please don't make the same mistake twice'.

Akio Morita

Example is leadership.

Albert Schweitzer

Gathering – a focusing exercise

This exercise gives participants the chance to share some of their personal qualities with the group. Each participant must complete the sentence '*I am someone who…*' – for example, 'I am someone who cares for other people and who is loyal to my friends and family.'

This connects with the theme 'Taking a Stand' on Day 3 of the Leadership Programme.

COMMENTS

The focus over the next two days is to raise participants' awareness of their own role within the group, of the workshop process as a whole, and of group dynamics. They need to start setting an example, supporting other participants and cooperating with the facilitators to help make the workshop a success. It is good to ask them questions that highlight aspects that help and aspects that hinder the learning process. Questions that examine the purpose of a specific exercise could also be asked. Encourage them to begin thinking about all the various aspects of the workshop – for example, the different exercises, the participation, the facilitation, the games, etc.

Trust Fall – a group trust exercise

This exercise works best with a larger group. You need a room with a high enough ceiling and a sturdy table that can safely hold the weight of one person. A participant stands on the table with their back to the group, who stand close behind them on the floor. The group stand together with their hands raised above their heads ready to catch the one who is falling. Taller participants stand closest to the table. When instructed, the participant falls backwards off the table, holding their body straight with their arms folded across their chest. The group catch the faller and lower them gently to the ground. They must be instructed and monitored carefully to ensure that no one gets hurt.

Feedback

Lead a discussion that focuses on teamwork and trust. Some useful questions are: 'What becomes available to all of us when people work together? Could you do this exercise on your own? Why not? In what areas of your life do you need this kind of participation from others? In what areas of your life do you need to participate with others? In what areas of your life do you need to trust others? When do you need this level of trust with others? What did people do or say in this exercise that made it easier for you to trust the group? What did people do or say in this exercise that made it more difficult for you to trust the group? What is the purpose of doing such an exercise? Has it worked today, has the purpose been achieved?'

Focus of the Day

Working with others: Working creatively with conflict – acknowledging mistakes

Link this to the feedback from the Trust Fall. Leadership exists within the context of community, working together with others. Encourage participants to think of what the community offers them. Focus on how we depend on others in many areas of our lives – for example, for our food supply, water, electricity, transport, etc.

Discuss aspects that are critical to the functioning of a healthy community, for example:

- the way in which we work together
- the way in which we trust one another
- the way in which our conflicts are resolved
- the way in which our mistakes are acknowledged.

You can use some of the quotes on page 147 in this discussion.

The exercises today focus on factors that help build a sense of community, and those that threaten the well-being of a community.

Building a Tower – a team-building cooperative exercise

Participants work in teams. Each team gets a pile of newspaper and a roll of masking tape. With these resources, they have to build a paper tower that:

- has only three points/legs touching the floor
- stands to a height of at least six foot/two metres
- is freestanding, and not attached to the floor, ceiling, furniture or any other object.

Give the teams five minutes to plan, and ten minutes to build. Each member must have a specific role within the team, and this must be decided while planning. You can decide whether participants may speak while they build, or whether they must build in silence.

Feedback

The feedback should focus on teamwork: what worked well, what didn't work well, and what they could improve on next time. Discuss building a community and embarking on projects together. Use the metaphor of building the tower to facilitate the discussion. If building the tower was an example of creating a project, or a community, what are the strengths and weaknesses of its structure? What does your experience now suggest you would need to consider? Focus the discussion on the planning process, the building process, the different roles and skills needed, attention to detail, the outcome, and the ability of a team to be flexible.

Three-Two-One – a listening exercise in pairs

Ask participants to think of a conflict in which they have been involved, either in the past, or an ongoing conflict, that has ended, or might end, in a destructive way. Ask them to think of the key points in their conflict and plan how to tell the story of what happened in three minutes.

Participants work in pairs. One starts, and has three minutes to speak about the conflict they have chosen. Their partner just listens and, at the end of three minutes, has two minutes to report back on what they have heard, selecting only the most important points.

After the report back, the partner whose conflict it was has one minute to confirm that it did not omit any crucial information.

The partners then swap roles and repeat the process.

Feedback

'In what way does listening link to leadership? In what way does clear communication link with leadership? What was good about using this listening and feedback structure? How was it helpful to the listener that you planned and organised what you were going to say?

Comments

The aim here is to focus the participants on a specific conflict; to practise focused listening; to work on being able to extract key information and report back; and to focus on how people feel when they have been listened to, and when they know that what they have said has been heard. This is the best way to create a sense of community, which is an essential quality to develop in a team.

Game

Choose a game that is fun and relaxing.

Playing with Fire – a group exercise exploring conflict and using freeze-frame technique

In small groups, the participants select one of the conflicts that they shared in the previous exercise. Ask the group to brainstorm what they think each of the following six captions represents in the build-up to a conflict:

1. The fuel
2. The spark
3. Smouldering
4. Fanning the flames
5. Stoking the fire
6. The blaze.

Refer to the 'Fire and Conflict' graphic opposite, and the accompanying table on page 153. Ask each group to divide the story of their conflict into six frozen pictures, corresponding to the sequence above. They should depict an incident that has developed all the way through to a 'blaze'.

Each group then shares their six pictures with the whole group. The member whose incident it was explains who is in the picture, and what each scene represents. With each scenario, the group explores the points at which the conflict escalated, and what caused this escalation. They also identify moments where an intervention could have been made to resolve or de-escalate the conflict, and discuss what kind of intervention it might have been.

You might ask them to transform a particular picture into what they would ideally like it to be, and then chart the journey that would lead from the original picture to the desired picture. Ask them what it would take to make each part that journey. What support would they need?

Feedback

Feedback questions could focus on the benefits of separating the stages in a conflict, and dividing up the issues and dynamics involved into manageable parts.

FIRE AND CONFLICT

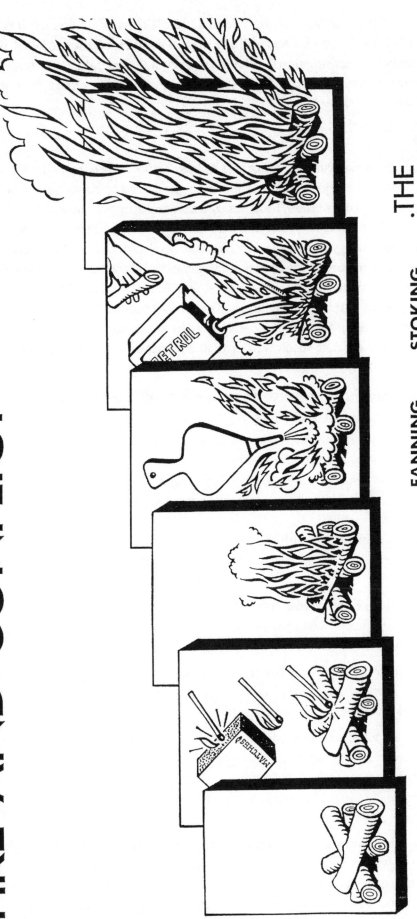

.THE FUEL.   .THE SPARK.   .SMOULDERING.   .FANNING THE FLAMES.   .STOKING THE FIRE.   .THE BLAZE.

'How have you found this 'Fire and Conflict' model useful? How could you use it with others who are in conflict? What roles can leaders usefully play in conflict situations? What *skills* could be useful to help resolve conflict situations? What *qualities* could be useful to help resolve conflict situations? What interventions that have been suggested during this exercise have you found useful?'

COMMENTS

The aim here is to increase participants' awareness of how conflicts develop and escalate, and to focus on points and methods of intervention. This training will need to continue and be practised throughout the Leadership Programme. The aim is to train participants in intervention techniques that they can apply with their peers, to take the lead in resolving disagreements and disputes.

The 'Playing with Fire' analogy can be used to plot the development of a short-term conflict – such as a disagreement that happened the previous day and lasted for an hour or the whole day – or to analyse a long-term conflict that began, for example, in childhood and continues into adulthood.

The six stages suggested in this exercise, from 'The fuel' all the way to 'The blaze', could also be used as a metaphor to help plan a project, a campaign or an event. It could be used for leading a build-up to a positive and creative result, rather than a negative, destructive conflict.

Support Yourself – an individual exercise focusing on acknowledging mistakes

One of the ways in which we undermine ourselves and the communities we live in is to deny or ignore the mistakes that we have made. When others do not acknowledge mistakes they have made, it tends to create rather than reduce conflict.

Ask each participant to think of a mistake they have made – for example, 'I said I would visit my mother, but didn't turn up when she was expecting me. I know she is mad with me. I haven't spoken to her or been home since.'

Take some of the participants through the following process and give examples at each stage to help them grasp the difference between handling a mistake responsibly and avoiding all responsibility.

1. **First, acknowledge what you have done** – *for example*, 'I arrived one hour late for work today,' *rather than* 'I wasn't really late. I was only a little late. Anyway, people are always coming late.'

2. **Second, accept responsibility for it** – *for example*, 'Yes, I am responsible for getting to work on time,' *rather than* 'It's my alarm clock. It never works. If it wasn't for my alarm clock, I would have been at work on time.'

3. **Third, clean up what you have done**. That is: clear up the mess, have any conversations you need to have, do what you need to do – *for example*, 'I need to apologise to my supervisor and colleagues for being late. I will offer to make up the work I missed during my lunch break,' *rather than* 'I have nothing to apologise for. I told you it was my alarm clock. I'm not to blame. There is nothing for me to make up. Forget it, I'm not doing anything.'

4. **Fourth, see what you can do to make sure it does not happen again** – *for example*, 'I will buy a new alarm clock. I will always check that it is working. I will keep a spare battery for it just in case,' *rather than* 'On the wages they give me I can't afford a good alarm clock. What do they expect? If they want me at work on time *they* can go and buy *me* an alarm clock.'

Fire: conflict and change

Conflict

PEOPLE

Whenever people are in contact with each other, there is potential for conflict. This potential will vary according to the different degrees of combustibility in the individuals.

INCIDENT

There are always tensions and disagreements between people. Some of them can cause a spark which ignites conflict.

BROODING

Tensions and grievances are smouldering away but are unexpressed. The conflict feeds off rumour and gossip.

AGGRAVATION

Those who are interested in agitating the situation provoke it further. Feelings of anger and hurt may be expressed as prejudice and hate.

ESCALATION

The situation is intensified by the outside pressures of the social environment. Prejudice and disaffection add to the conflict.

CONSEQUENCES

There is a blazing conflict in which some people are damaged. No-one involved is untouched by it.

Fire

THE FUEL

The raw material of the fire. Some of it is highly combustible. Some of it is damp and flame-resistant.

THE SPARK

Friction causes sparks to fly. Some land on dry wood and it catches light.

SMOULDERING

The fuel catches light and begins to smoke. There is an indication of fire.

FANNING THE FLAMES

The wind blows and the smouldering fuel flickers with life. The flames lick and leap.

STOKING THE FIRE

The fire consumes the fuel. It demands more. Huge logs are piled onto the fire.

THE BLAZE

The fire rages. It is a huge blaze. It will not die down easily.

Change

PEOPLE

Whenever people are in contact with one another, there is potential for challenge and growth. Different values, opinions or aims contain raw issues and fuel for fire.

FLASH OF INSIGHT

There are always raw issues in a community or relationship. Sometimes a flash of new insight can bring an issue alive for an individual.

TENTATIVE RESPONSE

The individual looks for shared concern from others, making an initial response to the issue.

ENCOURAGED ACTION

Those showing concern for the issue grow in number, encouraging and supporting each other.

INCREASED RESPONSE

Response to the issue increases. The possibilities of achievement inspire action from many.

EFFECTIVE ACTION

Aims are achieved. People celebrate the blazing fire. It is a beacon which lights, warms and inspires.

Ensure that the participants understand the difference between *being blamed* for something and *taking responsibility* for it.

Feedback

In feedback, concentrate on what this process has to offer them. 'In what ways have you found this process useful? Why is it important to handle mistakes that we have made? What do we normally do when we make mistakes? What happens when we do what we normally do? How is it different when we acknowledge what we have done and take responsibility for it?'

COMMENTS

Leadership is all about handling our mistakes. Being able to acknowledge mistakes, clean them up and move on is crucial to leadership and the creation of a community. When people deny their mistakes, they get stuck, relationships break down, and trust is broken. Taking responsibility for a mistake means being able to make a personal response to a situation, rather than waiting to see what will happen. By being responsible, by saying 'I did it, it was me,' you can deal with the incident. You are being proactive and not allowing others to take the initiative. When we avoid responsibility and are blamed for something, we normally react to the accusation by saying, 'It wasn't me, I didn't do it.' This makes it extremely difficult for us to deal with the mistake and creates the feeling of shouldering the blame, like carrying a burden. In this way the mistakes just get bigger.

Closing – a large-group reflection and feedback exercise

In closing, the participants could be asked to reflect on the questions:

- What have I discovered about handling mistakes today?
- What have I discovered about working with others today?
- What have I discovered about working with conflict today?

This is also an opportunity for participants to express anything they need to before leaving the workshop.

FINAL COMMENTS ON THE DAY

Leaders often have to deal with conflicts of one sort or another. Leaders make mistakes. Participants in this programme can potentially take a positive leadership role with their peers in resolving conflict. They can also become powerful role models by taking responsibility for their own actions. The more work you do with the group on working with conflict and dealing with mistakes, the more it will enhance their effectiveness and empower them to take leadership.

> *When the Master makes a mistake, she realises it. Having realised it, she admits it. Having admitted it, she corrects it. She considers those who point out her faults as her most benevolent teachers.*
>
> *Tao Te Ching*

> *Failure is only the opportunity to begin again more intelligently.*
>
> *Henry Ford*

Day 3

Focus: *You as a facilitator*

Taking a lead –
facilitating others – building community

Agenda

- Gathering
- Trust Lift
- Focus of the Day
- Hot Topics
- Hot Seat
- Facts and Feelings
- Game
- Boxing Ring
- Achievements
- Acknowledgements
- Pyramid of Hands
- Evaluation
- The Next Step
- Closing Ceremony

Quotes to introduce the day

A true leader must work hard to ease tensions, especially when dealing with sensitive and complicated issues.

Nelson Mandela, personal notebook, 16 January 2000

People seldom improve
when they have no other models
but themselves to copy.

Oliver Goldsmith

Great persons are able to do great kindnesses.

Miguel de Cervantes

Gathering – a focus exercise

Each participant in turn shares with the group the type of leadership qualities they will aim for. A powerful way to do this is to imagine they are already using those qualities, so ask everyone to start with 'I am a leader who…' and complete the sentence themselves – for example, 'I am a leader who listens carefully and involves others in decision-making.'

This continues the theme of 'taking a stand' on Day 3 of the Leadership Workshop. By committing themselves to these qualities in front of the whole group, the participants can get honest feedback and support from others. They can begin to see that who they say they are is important, that they are taken seriously, and they begin to believe in themselves and to live up to their claim.

To increase the challenge in this exercise, and if you think there is sufficient trust, you could ask participants to stand up in front of the group as they make their statement.

Trust Lift – a group trust exercise

One participant lies on their back on the floor, with arms folded across their chest. Three to four participants stand in a line on either side, close to the person on the ground. One participant stands at their feet, and another at their head.

All together, the participants lift the person on the ground up to shoulder height, and then up above their heads. They turn around 180 degrees and then slowly lower the person back down to the floor. Everyone should be encouraged to have a turn.

Again, this trust exercise should only be facilitated by an experienced instructor. It requires everyone to know their role, listen to instructions and follow them carefully. If you consider that all is safe, you could give individual group members a chance to call out the instructions for running the exercise. In this way they begin to take responsibility for the process.

Feedback

In feedback, focus on the support and trust given, the clarity of instructions, the teamwork and concentration needed. Facilitate the group to highlight the courage needed to agree to being lifted and carried by others, the feelings involved in allowing yourself to let go, as well as the experience of knowing that somebody else is putting trust and faith in you.

Focus on questions exploring what can be achieved with the right support, trust and courage. Focus on how support needs to be specific, precise and well-timed to be effective, as it is in the exercise. Ask the participants what they thought was possible for themselves when they were being carried at the top of the lift.

COMMENTS

This exercise provides a great metaphor for what can be achieved when there is a solid base of support under an individual. It also emphasises that the individual must be willing to let themselves be supported. The Trust Lift elicits absolute concentration and focus from all involved, as well as rigorous teamwork. It gives participants an opportunity to take leadership in calling out instructions and running the exercise.

Focus of the Day

You as a facilitator: Taking a lead – facilitating others – building community

The focus is on participants playing an active role in their communities, whether it is in their local area, inside a school or a prison, with peers or with the wider community. The focus is also on taking the initiative, being responsible for something, rather than 'being done to'.

Leadership statements (see page 62) and the quotes on page 156 could be helpful in introducing the focus.

On Day 3, participants work on developing facilitation skills for running small group discussions. Below are four specific skills that are needed to be able to do this effectively:

- **staying unhooked** – not getting pulled in to arguments and disagreements; not giving answers and solutions; keeping your own opinion in your pocket

- **remaining impartial** – not taking sides; keeping a balanced position; encouraging everyone to listen to one another

- **facilitating others** – letting everyone have a voice; including everyone; encouraging active participation

- **listening with care** – listening with all your senses; listening to everything that is being said; 'listening' also to what is not being said.

Hot Topics – an exercise to generate ideas

Ask the participants to think of discussion topics that would definitely cause disagreements, strong emotions, and split the group. Write these subjects down, sufficient to fill a large sheet of paper. (Check how many in the group would vote for or against any given topic, and only write down those that create a noticeable split the group.) Hot topics might include, for example: 'Bring back the death penalty' or 'All rapists should be sterilised'.

Hot Seat – a facilitation training exercise

Ask for one volunteer to begin a group discussion. Ask that person to select a topic from the previous brainstorm list that they feel strongly about, and on which they have clear views. The person in the 'hot seat' now has to present a short introduction to the rest of the group (about two minutes). In this time, they should give a balanced picture of the topic, create an interest in it, and encourage all participants to take part, whatever their views.

Once the two minutes are up, the group gives the presenter feedback on how well they did their job. Ask: 'Did the speaker's own personal views dominate their presentation? Did they present in such a way as to include everyone and stimulate open debate? '

Encourage all participants to attempt the exercise. They will get creative ideas from each other. Highlight the presentations that worked best. Ask: 'What made them work? What went wrong with those that didn't work so well?'

Create a positive climate in which participants are encouraged to give each other constructive feedback that encourages improvement.

Feedback

Questions could include: 'What feedback did you find useful, and why? What feedback was not helpful, and why? What did you learn about yourself from this exercise? What did you learn about facilitation from this exercise? What did you learn about handling tough conversations from this experience?'

COMMENTS

The training dimension of this exercise is as important in the facilitation as it is in the feedback. Participants get a chance to really look at what works in each other's facilitation and to practise giving constructive feedback on what worked and what didn't.

Facts and Feelings – a facilitation training exercise

Participants work in groups of three. One takes the role of speaker, chooses a topic that they feel strongly about from the brainstorm list, and speaks for about two minutes.

The other two group members take the role of listeners. One listens for all the *facts and issues* in what is said, and feeds those back at the end of the time. The other listens for all the *feelings and attitudes* expressed, and feeds those back. Once they are finished, they can all give each other feedback on how well they think they did. The participants then swap over. They should each get a chance to practise all three roles.

Feedback

In the whole group feedback, focus on the practical value of being able to listen out for, and tell the difference between, facts and feelings. Possible questions include: 'What is important in being able to differentiate between facts and feelings? Can you listen for both at the same time? What did you learn from doing this exercise?'

The feedback questions from 'Hot Seat' could be used again here.

COMMENTS

Remind participants of the work done in previous workshops around facts and meanings – for example, 'Getting Hooked' and 'Getting Unhooked' (see pages 68–70 and 81–82); 'Vicious Circle' (pages 87–90). Distinguishing between facts and feeling gives us a powerful way to listen and a clear method for giving feedback.

Game

Select an appropriate game to play.

Boxing Ring – a facilitation training exercise using role-play

We use a similar structure to that for the exercise on Day 3 of the Leadership Workshop (pages 91–93). However, the focus is now on facilitator training.

A participant (the 'challenger') must facilitate a small group discussion on one of the brainstorm topics. The challenger has at least two coaches for support. In the Boxing Ring, the challenger faces three to four 'opponents', who take part in the discussion.

Each opponent is given a specific task by a coach – for example, one is told to be very quiet and shy, another to be loud and always talking, another to be bored and always complaining, and another could be upset by the views being expressed.

As with the original 'Boxing Ring' exercise, the opponents test the skills of the challenger. Ultimately, however, they are there to support the challenger to practise and develop their facilitation skills, by providing just the right level of opposition. Follow all the procedures in the notes given on Day 3 of the Leadership Workshop.

Feedback

In the feedback, look for what worked and what did not work, and what could be improved. Encourage as many participants as possible to try out this exercise.

COMMENTS

Allow plenty of time for this exercise, to give all participants a good opportunity to face a specific challenge, and to receive feedback and support from the rest of the group. 'Boxing Ring' provides a very useful framework for facilitation training, and it can be used regularly during later stages of the Leadership Programme. It is ideal for practice and preparation purposes.

Achievements – a reflection exercise as part of completing the workshop

See the Leadership Workshop (page 95), and use the same process here. Encourage participants to reflect on what they said about themselves in the Gathering exercises on Days 2 and 3. Ask: 'How have you performed in this Leadership in Action Workshop? What have you achieved? What are you proud of? What would you like to continue practising and developing?' This could be done in pairs, or in small groups of four.

Acknowledgements – a group personal-feedback exercise as part of completing the workshop

Use the same procedure as described in the Leadership Workshop (page 95). Ask the participants to focus their feedback to each other on the theme 'taking a lead in life'.

Pyramid of Hands – a group feedback and closing exercise

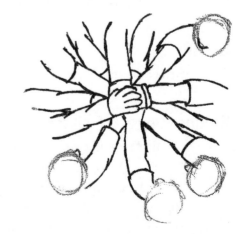

All participants stand in a circle. One at a time, they step into the centre of the circle and reach out with one arm, simultaneously declaring something they have appreciated about working as part of a team with all the other participants.

Once they have spoken, they keep their arm in that position. The next speaker then places their hand over the first speaker's hand, and so on, eventually forming a pyramid of hands. Encourage them not to leave people standing in the centre for too long, as it gets uncomfortable; they should step forward and make their contributions quickly.

Evaluation – a feedback exercise to use in completing the workshop

You can use exactly the same procedure as indicated at the end of the Leadership Workshop (page 95).

The Next Step – giving information and gathering ideas

The next steps depend on the roles you have developed for young people progressing through the programmes, but could include young people:

- supporting the delivery of the next Leadership Workshop, alongside the facilitation team
- delivering peer education/training workshops to other young people
- helping out in the youth centre or with activities in a school or college
- going on to further training, education or projects.

You will need to be clear with participants about the progression routes you are making available to them in your programme. They may need individual support and encouragement for making choices and accessing opportunities.

Closing Ceremony – completing the workshop

See the Leadership Workshop notes on page 95. Include certificates, a guest and a poem or piece of writing, as before.

The speakers this time could concentrate more on the theme of leadership, and give examples of what they, as well as others, have achieved in their lives by overcoming and rising above their circumstances or taking responsibility for themselves

---

FINAL COMMENTS ON THE DAY

A key Focus of the Day has been on listening and observing closely, as well as giving and receiving feedback. The participants have also had opportunities to practise some aspects of facilitation, particularly managing discussions and handling challenging situations. It should be stressed that this is only the first step in facilitation and leadership training. The learning process to gain experience, receive feedback and make the necessary improvements is a continuous cycle. Learning and training never stop. From now on the emphasis is no longer on workshops but on real-life, on-the-job training.

Success is sweet,
but it has the scent of sweat about it.

Anon

Some people see things as they are, and say, 'Why?'
I dream of things that never were, and say 'Why not?'

Ted Kennedy

Chapter 9

Fear and Fashion
Tackling Knife Carrying and Use

Introduction to the 'Fear and Fashion' Workshop

A commitment to non-violence is at the heart of Leap's approach. In Leap's view, carrying knives is unacceptable because of the increased risk of injury and harm, to the young person to themselves and/or others.

The 'Fear and Fashion' programme uses Leap's peer training/cascade model to train young people at risk of carrying and using weapons to deliver workshops for their peers on the issue of knife crime. The exercises in this workshop were developed from Leap's experience of delivering a partnership programme over three years in the Borough of Westminster, where there had been a number of serious woundings and a fatal stabbing involving young people.

The aim of these materials is to explore the causes and consequences of carrying and using knives. As in the Leadership in Action Workshop, the young people are being encouraged to 'turn outwards to examine this issue and its consequences for themselves and their communities. In order for young people to develop the skills to train others, they will need to participate in an adapted version of the Leadership in Action Workshop described in Chapter 8, incorporating some of the materials shared here.

Young people do not have to participate in the previous leadership workshops before undertaking this course. However, we recommend that they do. Previous participation in the Leadership Workshop will substantially deepen the level of engagement and learning for young people attending the 'Fear and Fashion' Workshop, as much of the content is underpinned by a need for self-leadership awareness and skills.

The training techniques used in this chapter are the same as those in previous chapters, but some of the exercises are unique, and others are adapted from other material specifically to explore issues around knife crime. Much of the material touches on issues of status, but a fuller exploration of these issues and those relating to power and reputation can be found in Leap's *Gangs Manual* (Feinstein and Kuumba 2006).

The workshop includes a range of techniques to explore the issue of knife crime. The starting point is an understanding of the context of knife crime, before the work moves on to explore the causes and consequences of carrying knives. Finally, the workshop shares a range of strategies to deal with conflict situations where knives may be used. Notes for facilitators will offer guidance on the delivery of the materials, and Part 1 of this book has explored in detail some of the wider issues around the delivery of this programme.

- **Day 1** explores the reasons why young people carry knives, by drawing out a range of different opinions and views, and encouraging participants to share their experiences with each other. It also examines who may be affected by the carrying and use of knives, and what happens when a serious incident occurs.

- **Day 2** focuses on choices and consequences, exploring how our choices in the moment can have unforeseen consequences.
- **Day 3** examines the notion of revenge, and supports participants in taking leadership on knife carrying and use with their friends, their peers and in the wider community.

Background to the 'Fear and Fashion' Project

The project name 'Fear and Fashion' comes from the findings of research carried out by Lemos and Crane (Lemos 2004) that highlighted these two factors as the main reasons why young people carry knives. 'Fear' refers to the decision to carry a knife for protection, believing that it will keep you safe if attacked. 'Fashion' refers to the decision to carry a knife to gain respect and status, and a desire to be 'one of the crowd'.

Media reporting of knife crime increased substantially between 2006 and 2008 and, ironically, may have contributed to young people's decisions to carry a knife or other weapon. Anecdotal evidence from young people and those who worked with them indicated to us that young people believed most of their peers were carrying knives, and that this contributed to their decision to do the same.

Leap's 'Fear and Fashion' Project worked in partnership with Westminster City Council from April 2007 to December 2010 to reduce violence, knife carrying and fear of violence in this specific London borough. The project took a two-pronged approach to achieving this aim: preventative training programmes in schools, and programmes in the community for young people at risk of involvement with knife crime. Both approaches followed the process described in earlier chapters of this book, in which young people undertake an intensive training programme that trains them to deliver workshops to their peers.

The funding for this programme has ended, but its legacy includes 20 peer educators who have trained over 700 of their peers on the causes and consequences of knife crime. Several of the peer educators have gone on to paid employment with the local authority. In addition, over 120 adult youth practitioners have been trained in techniques to tackle issues around knife crime.

Day 1

Focus: *Carrying knives*

Fear or fashion – me and others

Agenda

Session 1

- Introduction to the Workshop
- Personal Introductions
- Game
- Focus of the Day
- Where Do You Stand?
- Knife Wordstorm
- Fear and Fashion

Session 2

- Game
- Chain Reaction
- Who's Affected?
- Reflection Time
- Closing

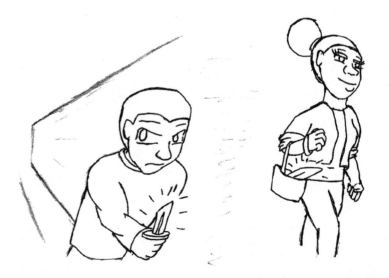

QUOTES TO INTRODUCE THE DAY

Two roads diverged in a wood, and I –
I took the one less traveled by,
And that has made all the difference.
  Robert Frost

The real act of discovery consists
not in finding new lands,
but in seeing with new eyes.
  Marcel Proust

The future depends on
what we do in the present.
  Mahatma Gandhi

Session 1

Introduction to the Workshop

Facilitators discuss the following points introducing the workshop theme. We suggest facilitators find an innovative way to introduce the workshop. Make sure you cover the following:

- introduce the facilitation team
- set the context: this might include any topical knife incidents or crimes; any current media or political attention; any accurate statistics regarding knife carrying or knife crime if they are available
- the background to working with this particular group – for example, the workshop may have either a 'preventative' focus (i.e. working with young people to discourage them from starting to carry knives) or a 'curative' focus (working with young people who are known to be carrying knives to explore the possible consequences of doing so)
- what the workshop will cover – exploring causes and consequences of carrying knives; developing strategies to deal with conflict situations where knives are carried; and understand the context of carrying and using knives.

Facilitators will also need to cover:

- what participants will do in the workshop
- the role of facilitators in the workshop
- how participants can get the most out of the workshop
- workshop guidelines for all to observe
- practical issues and housekeeping – times, breaks, meals, attendance, smoking, certificates, etc.

Refer to the Notes for Facilitators (on pages 53–56) and the introduction to the Leadership Workshop (on pages 57–58) for more ideas on how to introduce the workshop.

Personal Introductions – an introductory group exercise

Give each participant a chance to respond to the question 'What is your name and why have you chosen to attend this workshop?'

Game

Please refer to the other Leadership Workshops for games to help participants get to know each other and explore some of the themes of the workshop.

Focus of the Day

Carrying Knives: Fear or fashion – me and others

On this first day participants will be invited to examine their current thinking about carrying and using knives. Is it fear or fashion or a mixture of both? And what happens when a knife is introduced into a conflict situation? How does conflict escalate and who is affected?

The facilitators may want to link the focus to the issues raised by the participants in their personal introductions, and the issue of self-leadership. If you are making the decision to carry a knife out of fear or fashion, then who is leading you?

Where Do You Stand? – a large-group sharing exercise

Ask participants to stand up and move their chairs out of the space. Mark one end of the room 'Agree' and the other end 'Disagree'. The centre of the room is marked 'Not sure' – and so an invisible continuous line runs down the middle of the room.

Read out some or all of the statements listed below. For each statement, participants are asked to listen and then place themselves at the point of the invisible line that reflects their point of view. The statements are:

- Young people carry knives because it is fashionable.
- Anyone carrying a knife should get a prison sentence.
- If your friend is carrying a knife, you should tell an adult.
- People who carry knives are willing to use them.
- Adults are out of touch with how it really is for young people.

You may want to reword the statements to incorporate the language young people themselves would use. After each statement is read, the participants take up their positions. Ask a sample of the participants to say why they placed themselves where they did. Try and elicit a range of perspectives. Participants are allowed to move positions if they hear something that changes their opinion about one of the statements.

Feedback

The discussion should reflect on the content and the participants' experience of the exercise. Some questions to ask about the content are: 'What have you learned about knife carrying in this exercise? Whose concern is knife carrying?'

Some questions to ask about their experience are: 'What was it like to share your point of view or be listened to? Were you surprised about the different views in the group? Was it difficult to take up a different position from other people in the group? What was it like to be the only person standing in a particular position? What made you change your position? If everyone agrees, does that make it right?'

COMMENTS

This is a gentle way of introducing many of the aspects of carrying knives that will be looked at in more detail later during the workshop. The aim is to get the participants to vocalise their opinions and ideas and to highlight that knife carrying is a complex issue with many different perspectives, to be explored and challenged in further exercises. Facilitators might want to encourage some of the quieter participants to give their responses. It is important to encourage an atmosphere where everyone's views are shared and heard. It is also an opportunity to explore some of the themes around self-leadership that have been developed in the Leadership Workshop.

Knife Wordstorm – a whole-group exercise

Write the word 'knife' in the middle of a piece of flip chart paper. Ask the participants to call out all the other words they know for 'knife'. Now write 'damage' in the centre of a second piece of paper, and asks participants to name all the possible effects of using knives on another person. The normal wordstorming rules apply, in that participants should be encouraged to come up with as many words as possible and to take all contributions. When they have exhausted their suggestions, you can move into the feedback session.

(Examples of words for knives might be: *juk, slice, shank, shiv, blade, tool, tings*. Examples of words for damage might be: *maim, paralyse, damage, kill, death, scar, hurt, cut*.)

Feedback

Lead a discussion based on the following questions: 'Why have so many different words for knives evolved? Who creates this vocabulary? Why? How does it feel to use these words with your friends? Around adults?'

Comments

Young people create their own vocabulary as a way to reclaim some power in situations where they feel they have little control. The invention and use of this language can boost their status within their peer group, and distinguishes them from adults, who may not know the meanings of some of the words used by young people. It is also, however, a way to avoid naming what is really happening, and confronting the behaviour and its consequences.

Fear and Fashion – a tableaux exercise in small groups

Participants get into groups of three or four. Each group creates three tableaux:

- the first illustrates young people with knives
- the second shows the reasons why they are carrying knives
- the third demonstrates what is behind the reasons given in Picture 2.

For example, the first picture might depict a couple of young people comparing knives. The second picture might depict another group of young people who are also armed. The third picture might depict fear of being outnumbered.

The groups show their tableaux to the rest of the group. The audience can guess what each picture depicts, before the performers give an explanation.

To illustrate the connection between the three tableaux, three small groups each recreate one scene from one group's set of pictures. The first tableau is shown and then moves aside to reveal the second picture behind it, which in turn moves aside to reveal the third picture behind that.

Feedback

Focus the discussion on the underlying reasons why people carry knives. 'Why do people carry knives? What are the fears? Where do they come from? What fuels them? Where do you feel fear in your body? How might you feel carrying a knife?'

COMMENTS

Young people may be carrying knives for protection because they are fearful of being attacked, or about how they might defend themselves if they got into a fight. Or they may do it because it is fashionable – everyone else is doing it, and they want to be part of the in-crowd or fit in with their group. They may be coerced or manipulated into carrying a knife by older peers, a friend or boyfriend in order to lessen the risk of that person being caught. The increased media attention on knife carrying may highlight the need to address broader societal concerns, but it may also fuel these justifications for carrying weapons. Further exercises explore whether or not carrying a knife contributes to someone's safety.

You could relate this exercise to 'Vicious Circle' in Session 5 of the Leadership Workshop (pages 87–90). In Circle 1: 'What happened' you could refer to a local incident where a young person got stabbed. In Circles 2 and 3 you could explore the thoughts and feelings, and in Circles 4, 5 and 6 examine the actions, costs and benefits. This could lead to an interesting discussion about where the power lies.

Session 2

Game

Choose a game to play with the group.

Chain Reaction – a group role-play exercise

The facilitator asks six members of the group to volunteer to create a tableau of one young man knifing another in the leg, whilst four others look on. After the group has seen the tableau, the participants decide the names of the characters involved, what roles they took in the scenario, and why it might have happened. The facilitator asks the group to think about what might have happened to lead up to the scenario they have just seen; they will then develop three scenes that culminate in the incident shown.

The participants will work in groups of six, and each group will create four tableaux to represent each scene. Once the groups are ready, they show the whole group their scenes in chronological order. After each scene is shown back, the facilitator asks the participants the following questions:

- How do you think the characters feel?
- What made the situation get worse?
- Who could have made a difference?
- How can the harm be put right?

Feedback

'Who do you most identify with in the scenes: the protagonist, the person being attacked, the friends of the protagonist, or the friends of the person being attacked? Who did you identify with least? Why? What did the bystanders contribute to the conflict? At what points did the conflict escalate? At what points could someone have done something different that might have defused the situation?'

You can draw the diagram opposite. Identify the actions that escalated the conflict and write them up on the escalator. Ideas for de-escalating the conflict at each point can be written below the line. write in the points of escalation and ideas for defusing the conflict.

Sample scenario

Scene 1:   Dylan flirts with Sunita. Sunita is going out with Matthew.
Where: on the way to school
Who: Dylan and Sunita
Why: Dylan finds Sunita attractive.

Scene 2:   Matthew's friends tell him what happened on the bus.
Where: school grounds
Who: Matthew's mates and Matthew
Why: Matthew is their mate and they don't like Dylan.

Scene 3:   Matthew winds up Dylan and insults his mum.
Where: school grounds
Who: Matthew, Dylan and friends of both
Why: Matthew wants to show Dylan who is boss.

Scene 4:   Dylan has knifed Matthew in the leg.
Where: outside of school
Who: Dylan and Matthew
Why: Matthew showed Dylan up in the school grounds and Dylan wants revenge.

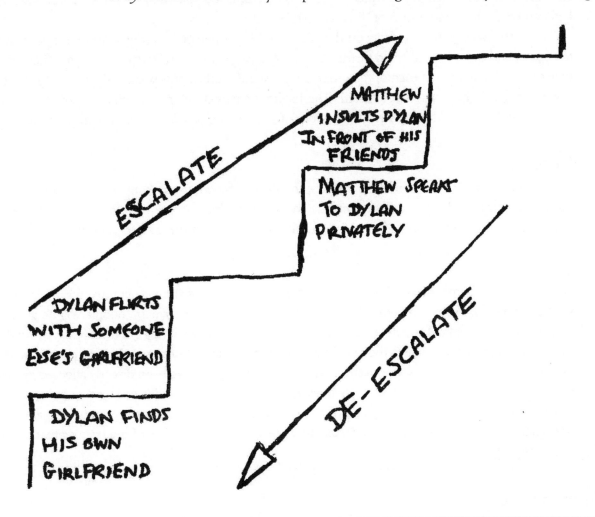

COMMENTS

Young people will often say they were bystanders, rather than protagonists or victims, in situations of knife crime. It can be argued, however, that a young person is involved in whatever is happening just by being there, and will often have to pay the consequences. This is also how the situation may be viewed from a legal standpoint. Bystanders also influence the protagonist and the victim, who may feel they have to act 'tough' in front of them. It is also important to draw a clear distinction between behaviours that escalate and behaviours that could defuse the situation. The concept of choices in difficult situations is developed further on Day 2 in 'Choices and Consequences'.

Who's Affected – a whole-group exercise

Stick together four pieces of flip chart paper to make a large rectangle, and place it on the floor. Draw a big dot in the centre, and the largest possible circle around it. The participants are told that this represents a fight between two young people where one young person has knifed and seriously wounded another.

In pairs, the participants make a list of all the people affected by the incident – for example, the young people involved, their friends, their families, the police, the ambulance service, any witnesses, etc. Each pair feeds back to the wider group, and each affected person or group is recorded in large letters on a separate, large strip of flip chart paper.

The participants place the strips on the circle – with the person or groups most affected nearest to the dot and those least affected further towards the edge of the circle. Participants are then asked to act as representatives of each of the groups. They stand on the appropriate strip and imagine how these people might have been affected. The facilitator taps different participants and they speak about how they were affected by the situation – for example, physically, emotionally, financially.

Feedback

'Were you surprised by the number of people affected by what has happened? Why was that? Were you surprised by the different effects the situation had on people? Why was that? What might you want to say to those involved in the fight, based on these observations?'

COMMENTS

Like the ripples from a stone thrown into a lake, the impacts of the incident are felt much more widely amongst friends, family and the wider community. In the aftermath, people will be affected in many different ways. The effects can be short-term, such as worrying about revenge or further attack, or longer-term, such as the fear of walking through an estate, or the dangerous reputation of a community affecting business in the area. Young people may have been directly affected by knife crime, and may have experienced family members, friends or their wider peer group being injured or harmed. This exercise can bring up powerful emotions or memories, and some participants may need individual support and a chance to talk to a key worker or member of the training team at the end of the day.

Reflection Time

An opportunity to reflect in pairs on the experiences of the day.

Closing – a whole-group reflection and feedback exercise

Please see the Leadership Workshop for ideas on how to close the day.

Day 2

Focus: *Choices and consequences*

The costs and gains of the choices I make

Agenda

Session 3

- Gathering
- Clearing
- Game
- Focus of the Day
- Choices and Consequences
- Consequences Tree

Session 4

- Game
- Court Case
- Reflection Time
- Closing

Quotes to Introduce the Day

One's philosophy is not best expressed in words, it is expressed in the choices one makes. In the long run, we shape our lives and we shape ourselves. The process never ends until we die. And the choices we make are ultimately our responsibility.

Eleanor Roosevelt

Keep away from people who try to belittle your ambitions. Small people always do that, but they really make you feel that you, too, can become great.

Mark Twain

The only journey is the journey within.

Rainer Maria Rilke

Session 3

Gathering – a large-group focus exercise

The participants are welcomed back to the workshop and asked to re-introduce themselves, saying their name and how they are feeling about being here today, as a way of checking in. One participant or facilitator will begin and the rest follow suit, round the circle.

Clearing – an exercise to reflect on the previous day

The facilitator should explain to participants that both Day 2 and 3 will start with a clearing. The purpose of a clearing is to 'clear up' anything from the previous day to ensure that everyone can participate fully today. Participants may want to clear up something between themselves and another participant or one of the facilitators, speak about how the previous day's work left them feeling, or declare any insights they had overnight. See the Advanced Leadership Workshop (page 115) for further details on clearings.

Game

Choose a game suited to the theme and Focus of the Day

Focus of the Day

Choices and Consequences: The costs and gains of the choices I make

The focus for Day 2 is to explore the concept of choice and the consequences of the choices that people make. In the heat of the moment, people may think they do not have many alternatives. There are always, however, different options to choose from, although decision-making is not necessarily easy.

Session 3 presents an opportunity to explore the range of choices in particular situations, and to weigh up those choices and see what outcomes they may lead to. Any decision will result in some outcomes or consequences – these may or may not have been intended and may well be out of the decision-maker's control.

In Session 4 participants take part in a simulation of the trial of a young man accused of a knife crime, and explores how the court system would deal with the offence.

You could use some of the quotes opposite to encourage a discussion around the focus for the day.

Choices and Consequences – a large-group role-play

Ask for a volunteer from the group. Tell them you will read out five stage directions for them to follow, and that they will need to follow the instructions. Assure them they will not be asked to do anything silly or embarrassing. Set up the stage with a chair and read out the instructions:

1. A young man is sitting at home watching the television.

2. His mobile phone rings.

3. He talks for a short while and then hangs up.

4. He goes into the kitchen and gets a knife.

5. He puts the knife inside his jacket and runs out of the house.

Ask the audience what they think is happening. For example, who might this person be? What do they think the person on the other end of the phone is saying? Where do they think the young man is going? Try and draw out the scenario that would involve a young man being called to back up his friends in a fight. Ask the audience to explore what they think the character might be thinking and feeling at different points in the scene. Ask them to think about what might have happened to lead up to the mobile phone ringing, and what could be the possible consequences of the young man leaving the house with a knife. Explore both positive and negative consequences.

Agree on a scenario, and ask for a second volunteer to play the role of the person making the phone call. The two volunteers are given two minutes to rehearse the conversation. The narrative is re-enacted, this time incorporating the phone call.

The audience is then told that they will see the scene for a third, and final, time. This time they can stop the action at any point they feel something different could happen. When a member of the audience stops the action, they are invited to offer their suggestion as to what could happen. You will need to take responsibility for facilitating this process. If appropriate you might ask someone who makes a suggestion to take the place of one of the volunteers to try out their strategy. When the narrative is re-enacted various endings are possible, based on the suggestions of the audience.

Feedback

Lead a discussion using the following questions: 'Who is responsible for making the choices in the original scenario? What choices did the young man have? Did the choices increase or decrease as the scenario developed? When the young man changed his behaviour, how did that affect the other character? Can we separate the consequences of our actions from our choices? What do we have control over: our choices or the consequences?

COMMENTS

At the heart of this exercise is the concept of thinking through the potential consequences of choices. When participants are asked why they behaved in a certain way, a common response is 'I had no choice'. This exercise helps to demonstrate that there are always choices, even though these choices may feel limited. In the narrated scene, for example, if the main character chooses not to back up his friend there are many possible consequences: he may not get back-up himself in a future situation; he may be ostracised by his group; or he may be respected for standing his ground. If the character chooses to back up his friend, he may get hurt; he may hurt someone else; and he may be arrested. The facilitator should point out that by making choices we are responsible for the consequences, even if they are not what we intended.

The aim is that, by exploring the potential costs and gains of each choice, the participants will be in a stronger position to make informed decisions about their behaviour.

If you have time you could examine the thought process that drives the young man to go to the drawer and pick up the knife, and examine the concept of choice from the basis of how he is choosing to interpret the initial information he hears in the phone call. For example, if his thought is 'I have to back up my friend, no matter what', that will restrict his choice in this situation.

This exercise follows on well from the exercises 'Insults and Accusations' and 'Getting Unhooked' in the Leadership Workshop (see pages 79–82).

Consequences Tree – a small-group exercise

This exercise builds on the work on consequences which was started in the previous exercise.

Ask participants to get into groups of three or four, and give each group a few sheets of flip chart paper. Refer them to the original scenario in 'Choices and Consequences' where the young man leaves his house with a knife. Starting from this point, ask each group to chart a 'consequences tree', which maps out what might happen if they go out with a knife. They might, for example, be stopped by the police; get into a fight; or not get caught. They then need to map out all the possible consequences from each of these options. What, for example, are the consequences of getting stopped by the police? They might be arrested; or make a run for it; or blame their friend. They continue this part of the exercise until they have followed all the consequences through to a final point.

You may want to give the participants an outline of what the tree might look like; an example from a previous workshop is illustrated overleaf.

Feedback

Using the consequences tree from one group, the facilitator asks: 'Which actions does the young man choose? Which consequences can he control? In terms of time-frame, how quickly do the consequences become out of his control? Which consequences might increase the young man's status or reputation? With whom? Which might decrease his reputation or status? With whom?'

COMMENTS

The intention of this exercise is to chart the chain of consequences that follow from making a particular decision, particularly once a young person attracts the attention of the police. By mapping them out, young people can see the chain of consequences that can follow from one action, most of which they have no control over. It could be argued that if you choose a particular course of action, such as carrying a knife, then you are also choosing the consequences of that action – whether you intended them or not. Whilst young people's status or reputation might increase within their own peer group when they become involved with the criminal justice system, it is likely to decrease among family and community members.

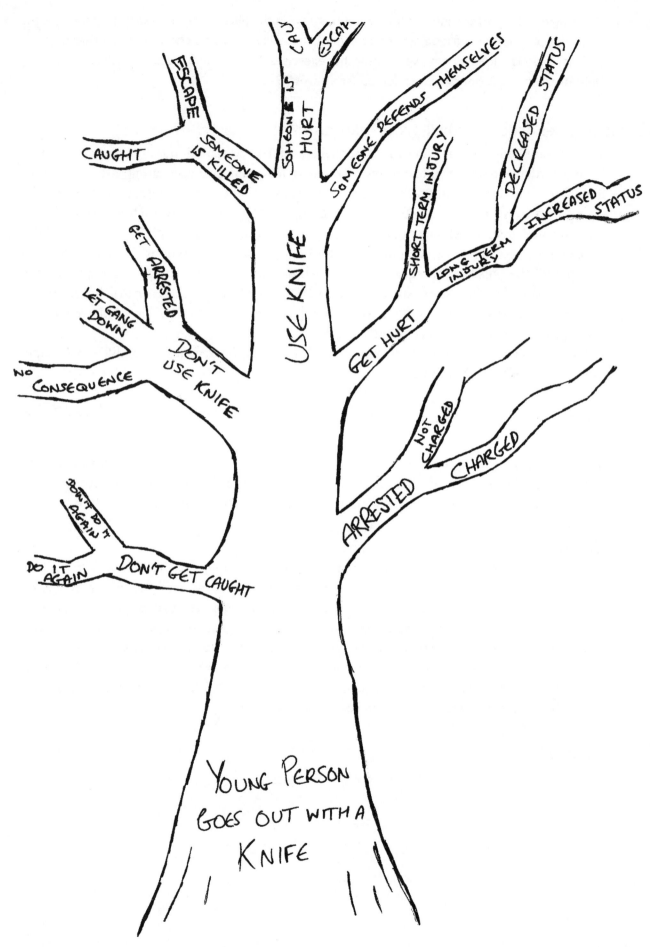

Session 4

Game

Choose a game to play with the group.

Court Case – a large-group simulation of a court case

This exercise gives participants an opportunity to create and participate in a mock trial, to experience how the criminal justice system works in practice; to explore the roles of the key players in the criminal justice system; and to see the possible outcomes of a court case.

Outline of the case:

> Vijay, an 18-year-old Asian student in his final year of 'A' levels, went out with a knife. He was on his way to the youth club that he attended twice a week. He had taken to carrying a knife because of a number of fights between some of his Asian friends and a gang of white young men from the neighbouring estate. He had not been involved in any fights, and had no intention of using his knife – indeed, he had not given the matter of carrying a knife much thought, except that it made him feel safer.
>
> Paul, a 24-year-old white man, and an accomplice, Jason, a 30-year-old white man, are repeat offenders. They regularly commit street robbery, stealing cash, credit cards, mobile phones and sometimes trainers, to sell to raise money to pay for drugs.
>
> Vijay took a short cut through the estate on which Paul lived because he was in a hurry; this was not something he normally did. Paul and Jason cornered him and asked for his mobile phone. Vijay panicked and tried to escape. Paul threatened him, and Vijay drew his knife. In the resulting scuffle between Vijay, Paul and Jason, Paul was seriously cut by the knife and later died in hospital.
>
> The incident was witnessed by Ivy Regis, who was coming out of her flat to walk her dog. She called the police on her mobile phone; when they arrived Jason told the police that Vijay had knifed Paul. Vijay ran away from the scene and went to his youth club, where he told his youth worker his version of events. His youth worker took him to the police station, where they were informed that Paul had died. Vijay was then arrested for Paul's murder.

Talk through the case with the group; depending on participants' knowledge, you may also need to explain how the court works and the roles of the players in a trial. Depending on the number of participants, ask for volunteers or allocate the following roles:

- Vijay – defendant
- prosecuting lawyer – acting for the state
- defence lawyer – acting for Vijay
- six-person jury
- judge
- witnesses for the prosecution: Jason, Mrs Ivy Regis
- witness for the defence: Vijay's youth worker.

If there are more participants, the facilitator can create more characters, such as Paul's mother, Vijay's father or teacher, the shopkeeper outside whose shop it happened, a journalist, ambulance staff, the police officer who made the arrest, and so on. They can create more details to bring the case and the characters to life.

Everyone has 20 minutes to prepare for the court case. Jason will work with the prosecuting lawyer to plan a four-minute speech for the lawyer to deliver to the court. Vijay will work with his defence lawyer to plan a four-minute speech that his lawyer will present to the court.

The jury needs to appoint a foreperson who will speak on their behalf. The other characters need to develop their characters' backstories and names, bearing in mind the sorts of questions they might be asked as witnesses in the case. It would be helpful for everyone to wear a label to identify their role in the case.

Set up a mock court with the judge at the front, facing everyone else; the jury in a line at right angles to the judge, on the judge's right; the lawyers facing the judge; and Vijay in the dock at right angles to the judge, on the judge's left. Witnesses sit outside the room until they are called to give evidence. The judge runs the session and will ask everyone in the court to identify themselves and explain why they are there.

The judge asks the prosecuting lawyer to present their case. Then the prosecuting lawyer can call the two witnesses for the prosecution to give evidence, starting with Jason. Each witness will be asked up to four questions. Once this had been done, the defence lawyer then has the right to cross-examine the witnesses and can ask them each up to four questions. The jury may not ask any questions.

Then the defence lawyer presents the defence for Vijay, who goes into the dock and is questioned by his lawyer. After that the prosecuting lawyer can cross-examine him by asking four questions. A similar process will happen with the defence witness, who is Vijay's youth worker.

The judge keeps control of time. After the witnesses have been questioned, the prosecutor and the defence lawyer can sum up their case; they have two minutes each.

The judge instructs the jury to retire to consider their verdict. The jury can remain in the room to do this, but must not speak to anyone else until they reach a verdict. Ideally they will reach a unanimous verdict. If they have not reached an agreement after 15 minutes the judge needs to let them know that a majority verdict (4:2) will be accepted, and gives them another five minutes. If they do not reach a verdict, it will be a mistrial and the case will need to start all over again at a later date. During this process, the other participants can observe the process the jury use and the roles the jury members take in reaching a decision.

The judge asks the foreperson of the jury to give the verdict and asks, is it a unanimous or majority verdict. If the offender is found guilty, the judge will need to consider what prison sentence to pass, and sentence him. If he is found not guilty, Vijay is free to leave the court.

Sentencing information: The judge must impose a mandatory life sentence for an offender found guilty of murder, and set a minimum term they must serve before they can be considered for release by the Parole Board. At the time of going to print, the starting point which would usually be applied where murder is committed with a knife or other weapon is 25 years' imprisonment. If released, an offender serving a life sentence will remain on licence for the rest of their life, and may be recalled to prison if they are considered a risk to the public (see www.sentencingcouncil. org.uk).

Feedback

What were people's experiences of the court process from the point of view of the offender, the victim, the lawyers, the witnesses and the jury members? Did participants think that the process was fair or not? Why is that? Did participants think it produced the right result? What was it like for jury members having to decide a verdict? What influenced their decision? What was it like being the judge and having to sentence the offender (if he was found guilty)? What do participants think about the current length of the sentence for murder committed with a knife? Would participants have felt differently if the crime had been pre-meditated rather than random?

COMMENTS

This is a very simplified version of a Crown Court trial. The aim is to give participants an experience of the criminal justice system and some of the dilemmas faced by those who operate within the system. It may also illustrate how people can describe the same event in different ways, according to the outcome they want. This exercise will need to be closely facilitated. It could be adapted for different offences.

It could also be useful to explore the different roles and who controls the outcome of the case.

Reflection Time

Provide an opportunity to reflect in pairs on the experiences of the day.

Closing – a whole-group reflection and feedback exercise

See previous workshops for ideas on how to close the day.

Day 3

Focus: *For the future – leading others*

The gamble of revenge or the chance for change?

Agenda

Session 5

- Gathering
- Clearing
- Game
- Focus of the Day
- The Gamble of Revenge
- Conversation with a Friend
- Just Say 'No'
- The Chance for Change

Session 6

- Game
- Campaign for Change
- Concentric Circles
- Evaluation
- Closing Ceremony

Quotes to Introduce the Day

Life is either a daring adventure or nothing.
Helen Keller

It is hard to fail, but it is worse never to have tried to succeed.
Theodore Roosevelt

Wherever we look upon this earth, the opportunities take shape within the problems.
Nelson A. Rockefeller

Session 5

Gathering – a whole-group focus exercise

See Session 3 on Day 2 (page 175).

Clearing – an exercise to reflect on the previous day

See Session 3 on Day 2 (page 175).

Game

Choose a game that fits with the theme and Focus of the Day.

Focus of the Day

For the future – leading others: The gamble of revenge – the chance for change

The main focus of Day 3 is the development of skills and techniques to enable young people to resist the urge to carry knives. They will practise strategies for handling a conversation with a friend who is considering carrying a knife, and non-violent methods for dealing with challenging situations. They will also devise a media strategy to encourage other young people not to take up arms. Apart from the consequences of becoming involved in the criminal justice system, young people involved in knife crime may also be subject to the 'street justice system' in the form of revenge from their peers. Session 5 starts with an exercise that explores how revenge works.

You could use the quotes on page 183 to encourage a discussion around the focus for the day.

The Gamble of Revenge – a paired tableaux exercise

Write the word 'Revenge' in the middle of a flip chart and ask participants to call out their thoughts about what the word means to them. They record the answers on the flip chart. They then wordstorm different types (actions) of revenge.

Encourage the group to think of both minor and major forms of retribution and record these on another sheet of the flip chart.

On a third sheet, the group wordstorms the feelings and needs associated with the act of revenge. Ask the group for any reflections on the ideas they have come up with. The group then picks six examples of revenge, ranging from minor to major, and lists them in order of severity; for example:

- blanking or excluding someone
- insulting someone in public
- threatening to attack with a knife
- stealing property such as an I-phone
- grassing
- group attack with a knife.

The participants are then divided into pairs, in which they choose whether to be Player 1 or Player 2. Each pair is given a set of scenario cards (see opposite) and two dice. Player 1 picks up a scenario card that describes what has happened to them, and reads it out loud. Player 1 then rolls the dice. The number that comes up decides the type of revenge Player 1 must take, and they create a tableau image of the revenge they carry out.

Player 2 then rolls the dice. The number the dice lands on determines the level of revenge they will in turn take on Player 1. They create a tableau image of the revenge they could carry out in retaliation for Player 1's action.

Bring the pairs back together and ask each pair to share their tableaux with the group. You can use the 'touch and tell' technique (see 'Who's Affected', pages 171–172) to invite participants to talk about their feelings and thoughts in the tableaux.

Feedback

What did it feel like in the moment in the tableaux? What power or control does someone have over the revenge that another person takes against them? Is it okay to take revenge? Why? What unwritten rules do participants have about taking revenge, or about appropriate levels of revenge? Does taking revenge always end the conflict? What other consequences might there be from taking revenge? What feelings and needs are associated with taking revenge?

How else could those needs be met? What are the alternatives to revenge that would allow people to keep their high status or reputation?

COMMENTS

On Day 2 participants explored the consequences of getting caught up in the criminal justice system. Whether or not that is one of the consequences of their action, people may also be subject to retribution or revenge after an incident or when they return to their community after a prison sentence.

Unwritten rules are rules that we live by, but which we do not necessarily articulate or question. For example, an unwritten rule may be that you always take revenge if you are slighted. In the moment of taking revenge, someone may feel very powerful. The act of taking revenge, however, often results in loss of power, because control then passes to the other person. What also happens with revenge is that the stakes tend to rise, often resulting in serious injury.

Revenge is tied up with issues of status and reputation, and not taking revenge can be considered a weakness.

This exercise relates to much of the material in the Leadership and Advanced Leadership Workshops – in particular, 'Vicious Circle' in the Leadership Workshop, where revenge can create a vicious circle that becomes increasingly difficult to break as the stakes rise, and the work on Acts in the Advanced Workshop. When taking revenge is about maintaining status or reputation, it is often because we are inhabiting one of our Acts. In order to make a different choice, a young person will need to choose to give up the Act.

'Gamble of Revenge' scenario cards

Scenario 1

Your phone was stolen from you on the street by a young man you have seen around.

Scenario 2

A local young person has been taunting your Mum as she walks through the estate.

Scenario 3

A group of young people you have not seen before walk past you, and one of them barges you in front of your girlfriend.

Scenario 4

You're walking alone down the street and three young people pass you and laugh at your trainers.

Scenario 5

You're threatened with a knife because someone you know said you'd grassed them up to the local shopkeeper for nicking stuff.

Scenario 6

You're attacked by someone your friend abused at the football a few weeks back.

Conversation with a Friend – a paired exercise that explores strategies

Ask participants what strategies they could use to talk a friend out of deciding to carry a knife. Record these on the flip chart. Ask participants to pair up. Each participant will get an opportunity to have a conversation with a friend who is, or is on the verge of, carrying a knife. The aim of the conversation is to try to talk their friend out of it. They can use any of the strategies or ideas listed on the flip chart, or any other ideas they have.

The pairs decide who will go first. The first protagonist says that they are going to start carrying a knife as there has been a lot of gang violence near their school. Allow five minutes for the exchange.

The pairs then swap roles. This time the protagonist states that they have been asked by their boy/girlfriend to carry a knife for them because the latter is potentially in danger.

Feedback

'What did it feel like trying to get a friend to change their mind? Is it the role of a friend to get their friends to change their behaviour? Which strategies were effective? Which were not effective? Who else could have this conversation with the potential knife carrier?'

COMMENTS

Persuading a friend not to carry a knife could be very challenging for a young person. By having an opportunity to share their ideas and fears, as well as to practise having a conversation with a peer, a young person can develop their ability and confidence to challenge their friend's behaviour. You could ask the participants to come up with a list of 'top tips' for talking to their friends. This could include such ideas as: allowing your friend a chance to explore and explain, by listening; speaking for yourself rather than telling your friend what to do; giving examples to illustrate what you are saying, etc.

Just Say 'No' – a small-group role-play exercise

This exercise asks the young people to apply their learning from the previous exercise. It gives them an opportunity to practise saying no to carrying knives. Ask the group what challenges they might have to deal with in relation to knife carrying – for example, being asked to keep a knife for someone else; being telephoned to give back-up; or being stopped by the police when you are with someone carrying a knife who tries to implicate you. Draw up a list of scenarios.

The participants will work in groups of four and pick one of the scenarios. One person will face the challenge; another will be the person challenging them. The other two people will play their thoughts. The role-play follows the following repeated pattern: the challenger's thoughts are voiced first, then the challenger speaks; next, the thoughts of the person facing the challenge are voiced and finally, they speak. Initially this will feel a bit unwieldy for the participants, but after some practice the process will flow.

The intention is to represent the inner dialogue that will be happening for each of the young people. The speakers can choose whether or not to act on their thoughts. The aim is for the challenged young person *not* to agree to do what their friend requests.

You could allow the dialogue to run for a few rounds; if there is time, allow the participants to swap roles, so that the 'thoughts' get a chance to play the speakers.

Here is an example of how the exercise might work:

1. **Challenger's thoughts:** 'I'm being targeted by the police; I need to get rid of my knife for a while, just in case.'

2. **Challenger speaks:** 'I need a favour for a couple of days – can you take this knife, just whilst the heat is on me?'

3. **Young person's thoughts:** 'Oh, no, I'd be an idiot to do this for him, but he is my mate and if I don't, he'll see me as a loser.'

4. **Young person speaks:** 'I am not sure if I can. Why don't you ask Marvin?'

Feedback

'How easy was it to resist the challenge of your friend? What made it difficult? What made it easier? Which thoughts were most powerful? Which thoughts hooked you in? What helped you unhook yourself? What helped you stick with your decision?'

COMMENTS

This exercise enables the participants to understand that you can choose whether or not to act on your thoughts. The stakes may be high for the young person: to some extent they are having to choose between the safety of being a member of their peer group, and keeping safe from becoming involved in the criminal justice system. They will need to be absolutely clear that they do not want to get involved, as their friends, in desperation, are likely to be very persuasive. This exercise develops the work on thoughts in the leadership work to deal with a specific situation such as being asked to carry a knife.

The Chance for Change – a group exercise to develop strategies

Ask the group what situations they might have to deal with in relation to carrying knives – for example, being asked to keep a knife for someone else, or being stopped by the police when you are with someone carrying a knife. Draw up a list of scenarios and ask the group to prioritise those that feel most relevant to them.

The group uses the 'Boxing Ring' format (see pages 91–93) so that one or two of the participants have the opportunity to face a challenge in the Boxing Ring.

Feedback

In addition to the feedback questions outlined opposite, ask: 'How has participating in this exercise shaped your thinking about knife crime? How confident do you feel having these conversations? What do you think could be the impact of having these conversations?'

COMMENTS

Issues relating to friendships and status are likely to be raised in this exercise. Challenging peers on their decisions can be a difficult thing to do, and this exercise enables participants to practise these conversations in a safe space. In addition, by witnessing the role-play of their peers in difficult conversations, participants further their understanding of their peers' thoughts and feelings about knife crime.

Session 6

Game

Choose a game to play with the group.

Campaign for Change – a small-group exercise to explore using the media to campaign against knife carrying

Ask the participants to get into groups of four. Each group can choose either modern media or more traditional forms of communication, to design part of a campaign to discourage other young people from carrying knives. They could, for example, write a song to upload onto MySpace; create a poster or banner to carry on the streets; or design an advertisement for the print media or television. They will have 25 minutes to create their campaign and will then show the results to the whole group.

Feedback

Which campaigns were most effective? Why was this? What is the key message participants wanted to get across to other young people? How else could this message be communicated?

COMMENTS

Young people are often better placed to influence other young people with regard to their behaviour than adults. They will also know how to use the relevant medium – for example, YouTube could be used to profile anti-knife crime messages through video; Facebook could be used to start a campaign.

Concentric Circles – a paired listening exercise to reflect on the experience of participating in the workshop

This exercise needs an even number of people sitting in a large circle. Ask participants to number off in pairs: one, two, one, two, etc. Ask all the 'ones' to stand up and turn their chairs round to face a 'number two', thus forming a circle inside a circle. They then sit on their chairs, each facing a partner.

Read out a question from the list below: the inside person will take two minutes to respond to the statement, whilst the outside person listens. They then swap roles, and the outside person has two minutes to speak to the statement while the inside person listens. You will need to keep accurate time.

Those in the inner circle then stand and move one seat to their right. Read out the next statement, and the process is repeated. At the end of this round the participants in the outside circle stand and move one seat to their left.

- How has your thinking about the pros and cons of carrying knives changed during the workshop?
- Would you intervene if you knew a friend was carrying a knife?
- What ideas do you have about how to prevent knife crime?

- Can you identify two actions you could take personally to minimise or prevent an increase in knife crime?
- If you had a message for other young people relating to carrying knives, what would it be?

Feedback

At the end of the exercise, ask people to feed back their ideas about preventing knife crime, and also to identify one action they personally could take to minimise or prevent knife crime.

COMMENTS

It is important to support and affirm participants' ideas – and, where possible, to ask them what their first step might be. The structure of this exercise is the same as 'My Life' on Day 1 of the Leadership Workshop (see page 64 for further details).

Evaluation – an individual exercise to feed back their experience of the workshop

This is an opportunity for the participants to give the facilitators feedback about their experience of the workshop. This is most usefully done as a written exercise, provided the participants do not have any difficulties with writing. You should already have prepared an evaluation form earlier, which asks the participants to score how well the learning outcomes have been met on a scale of 1–10, with 1 being 'not met at all' and 10 being 'completely met'. Allow space for any relevant comments after each grading.

Closing Ceremony – completing the workshop

See the closing ceremony for the Leadership Workshop (page 95). Include certificates, a guest, and a poem or piece of writing, as before. The speakers could focus on the benefits of giving up carrying knives and give examples of what they, as well as others, have achieved in their lives by overcoming and rising above their circumstances.

Resources

Organisations

- **Leapconfrontingconflict.org.uk**
  Offers training programmes and resources for working with young people and for conflict, and the adults who work with them.

- **www.theatreoftheoppressed.org**
  This site covers the range of theatrical forms that were elaborated and developed by the Brazilian theatre practitioner Augusto Boal in the 1950s and 1960s.

- **www.geesetheatre.com**
  Geese Theatre is a drama theatre company developing experiential theatre and therapy in 42 states and nine countries. Their site provides a valuable resource for training in drama therapy in prison, for correctional staff, sexual offenders, violent offenders, juveniles and adults, and theatre for prisons across the globe.

- **www.youthatrisk.org.uk**
  Youth at Risk is a charity dedicated to making a difference in the lives of vulnerable and disaffected young people. This site gives more details of their programmes and work with young people.

Bibliography

Anthony, R. (2011) *The Secret of Deliberate Creation.* Available at http://www.thesecretofdeliberatecreation.com, accessed on 19 May 2011. © Dr Robert Anthony 2011.

Baime C., Brookes, S. and Mountford, A. (2002) *The Geese Theatre Handbook.* Winchester: Waterside Press.

Benson, J (1997) *Working more Creatively with Groups.* London: Routledge.

Boal, A. (1985) *Theatre of the Oppressed.* New York, NY: Theatre Communications Group.

Boal, A. (1992) *Games for Actors and Non-actors.* London: Routledge.

Feinstein, J. and Imani Kuumba, N. (2006) *Working with Gangs and Young People.* London: Jessica Kingsley Publishers.

Freire, P. (1972) *Pedagogy of the Oppressed.* Harmondsworth: Penguin.

Goleman, D. (2005) *Emotional Intelligence.* London: Bantam Books.

Harrison, R. and Wise, C. (2005) *Working with Young People.* London: SageBannister.

Herrmann, A. and Clifford, S. (1999) *Making a Leap – Theatre of Empowerment.* London: Jessica Kingsley Publishers.

Hogan, C. (2002) *Understanding Facilitation: Theory and Principle.* London: Kogan Page.

Johnson, D.W. and Johnson F.P. (2005) *Joining Together: Group Theory and Group Skills.* London: Pearson/Allyn and Bacon.

Jones, P. (1996) *Drama as Therapy, Theatre as Living.* London: Routledge.

Lemos, G. (2004) *Fear and Fashion: The Use of Knives and Other Weapons by Young People.* London: Lemos & Crane

Macbeth, F. and Fine, N. with Broadwood, J., Haslam, C. and Pitcher, N. (2011) *Playing with Fire: Training Those Working with Young People in Conflict.* London: Jessica Kingsley Publishers.

Pascale, R. and Miller, A. (1998) 'Acting your way into a new way of thinking.' *Leader to Leader 1998*, 9, 36–43.